WHAT IS THE BOOK OF JUDGES?

Kids' Guides to God's Word Series

What Is the Book of Genesis?
What Is the Book of Exodus?
What Is the Book of Leviticus?
What Is the Book of Numbers?
What Is the Book of Deuteronomy?
What Is the Book of Joshua?
What Is the Book of Judges?
What Is the Book of Ruth?
What Is the Book of 1 Samuel?
What Is the Book of 2 Samuel?
What Is the Book of 1 Kings?
What Is the Book of 2 Kings?
What Are the Books of 1–2 Chronicles?
What Are the Books of Ezra & Nehemiah?
What Is the Book of Esther?
What Is the Book of Job?
What Is the Book of Psalms?
What Is the Book of Proverbs?
What Is the Book of Ecclesiastes?
What Are the Books of Song of Songs & Lamentations?
What Is the Book of Isaiah?
What Is the Book of Jeremiah?
What Is the Book of Ezekiel?
What Is the Book of Daniel?
What Are the Books of Hosea–Micah?
What Are the Books of Nahum–Malachi?

What Is the Gospel of Matthew?
What Is the Gospel of Mark?
What Is the Gospel of Luke?
What Is the Gospel of John?
What Is the Book of Acts?
What Is the Book of Romans?
What Is the Book of 1 Corinthians?
What Is the Book of 2 Corinthians?
What Is the Book of Galatians?
What Is the Book of Ephesians?
What Is the Book of Philippians?
What Are the Books of Colossians & Philemon?
What Are the Books of 1–2 Thessalonians?
What Are the Books of 1–2 Timothy & Titus?
What Is the Book of Hebrews?
What Is the Book of James?
What Are the Books of 1–2 Peter & Jude?
What Are the Books of 1-3 John?
What Is the Book of Revelation?

What Is the Book of
JUDGES?

Michael Whitworth

ISBN 978-1-971767-00-0

Published by Start2Finish
Bend, Oregon 97702
start2finish.org

Printed in the United States of America

30 29 28 27 26   1 2 3 4 5

CONTENTS

Introduction   7

1. The Generation That Forgot   13

2. The Cycle Begins   27

3. The Women Who Won the War   39

4. The Reluctant Hero and the Bramble King   51

5. The Outcast and the Terrible Promise   65

6. The Strongest and the Weakest   79

7. When Everyone Does Their Own Thing   93

8. Rock Bottom   107

INTRODUCTION

Have you ever watched a movie where you wanted to yell at the screen? You know the kind. The character is about to walk into an obvious trap. The villain is clearly lying. The "friend" is obviously going to betray them. And you're sitting there thinking, *Don't do it! Can't you see what's happening?*

But they do it anyway. Every single time.

That's basically the experience of reading the book of Judges. For roughly three hundred years, the people of Israel made the same mistakes over and over again. They forgot God. They worshiped idols. They suffered the consequences. They cried out for help. God rescued them. Things were good for a while. And then—you guessed it—they forgot God and started the whole cycle again.

It's frustrating. It's maddening. And it's one of the most important books in the entire Bible.

WHY JUDGES MATTERS

If you've grown up in church, you probably know some of the famous stories from Judges. Gideon and his fleece. Samson and Delilah. Maybe you've heard about Deborah, the woman who led Israel into battle, or Ehud, the left-handed assassin who killed a very fat king (yes, that's really in the Bible).

But here's the thing: most people only know these stories as isolated Sunday school lessons. They miss the bigger picture—the thread that ties all these wild tales together and explains why they matter.

The book of Judges isn't just a random collection of action stories. It's a carefully crafted argument. The writer wants to show you something. He wants you to see what happens when people abandon God and decide to live however they want. He wants you to feel the downward spiral, to watch things get worse and worse, until you're crying out along with Israel, "We need a king! We need someone to save us!"

And that's exactly the point.

Judges sets up everything that comes after. Without Judges, you can't fully understand why Israel wanted a king so badly. Without Judges, you won't appreciate how different David was from the leaders who came before. And without Judges, you'll miss one of the clearest pictures in the Old Testament of why we need Jesus.

WHAT YOU'RE ABOUT TO READ

Let me give you a quick roadmap of where we're headed.

The book of Judges covers the period between Joshua's death and the rise of the kings like Saul and David. Joshua had led Israel into the Promised Land. They had won great victories. Everything seemed to be going well. But Joshua warned them: if they forgot God and started worshiping the idols of the nations around them, disaster would follow.

Spoiler alert: they didn't listen.

The first section of Judges (chapters 1–3) shows us how Israel's faithfulness began to crumble. They didn't finish what they started. They let the Canaanites stick around. They intermarried with them. They started worshiping their gods. And before long, they had completely forgotten the Lord who rescued them from Egypt.

The middle section (chapters 3–16) tells the stories of the judges themselves. These weren't judges like the ones in courtrooms today. They were more like military leaders or deliverers—people God raised up to rescue Israel from their enemies. Some of them, like Othniel and Deborah, were pretty solid. Others, like Gideon and Jephthah, were more complicated. And Samson? Samson might be the most frustrating character in the whole Bible—a man with unlimited potential who wasted almost all of it.

What's really interesting is that the judges get worse as the book goes on. The first judge, Othniel, is basically a model hero. By the time we get to Samson, the "deliverer" can barely deliver himself. The downward spiral isn't just happening to Israel—it's happening to their leaders too.

The final section (chapters 17–21) shows Israel at rock bottom. There are no enemy armies in these chapters. No foreign oppressors. Just Israelites doing terrible things to each other—making their own gods, destroying their own cities, kidnapping their own people. The book ends with one of the most haunting sentences in Scripture: "In those days Israel had no king; everyone did what was right in his own eyes."

A WORD BEFORE WE BEGIN

I need to be honest with you: Judges is not an easy book. It's violent. Really violent. People get stabbed, burned, dismembered, and worse. Some of the "heroes" do things that make you cringe. And the final chapters contain some of the darkest material in the entire Bible.

Why would God include this stuff in Scripture?

Because the Bible isn't a collection of fairy tales with nice, clean morals. It's the true story of what happened—and what happened was often ugly. God doesn't airbrush his people's failures. He shows us exactly how bad things can get when we turn away from him. He lets us see the consequences of sin in all their horror.

But here's the good news: even in the darkest parts of Judges, God never gives up. He keeps rescuing his people even when they don't deserve it. He keeps working even when they've forgotten him. His grace is more stubborn than Israel's sin.

And that's really the point of the whole book. Judges isn't ultimately about the judges. It's about the God who keeps saving his people despite their constant failures. It's about grace that won't let go.

ONE MORE THING

As you read through this book, you're going to notice a phrase that keeps coming up: "Everyone did what was right in his own eyes."

That sounds pretty good at first, doesn't it? Freedom! No rules! Everyone gets to decide for themselves!

But watch what happens when people actually live that way.

Watch the chaos. Watch the cruelty. Watch everything fall apart.

The book of Judges is an ancient argument against an idea that's very popular today—the idea that you should "follow your heart" and "be true to yourself" and "live your own truth." Judges shows us where that road leads. It's not pretty.

What Israel needed—what we all need—is not the freedom to do whatever we want. We need a King worth following. We need someone whose commands are actually good, whose ways actually lead to life, whose rule actually brings peace.

Israel was waiting for that King. They didn't know it yet, but the whole story was leading toward him. And many centuries later, he finally came.

But that's getting ahead of ourselves. First, let's go back to the beginning—to the generation that forgot.

Turn the page.

1

THE GENERATION THAT FORGOT

If you've seen *The Lion King*, you know what happens to the Pride Lands after Mufasa dies.

Under Mufasa's reign, the Pride Lands were thriving. The grass was green, the watering holes were full, and the animals lived in peace under the shadow of Pride Rock. Mufasa was a wise and powerful king who understood his responsibility. He taught young Simba about the Circle of Life, about how everything was connected, about how a true king serves his kingdom rather than himself.

Then Mufasa was killed. And Simba—the rightful heir—ran away.

What happened next was devastating. Scar took over, and the hyenas moved in. The once-beautiful Pride Lands turned into a wasteland. The herds left. The water dried up. The land that had been so full of life became gray, barren, and dead. When Simba finally returned years later, he barely recognized his home. Everything his father had built was gone.

There's a moment in the movie when Mufasa's ghost appears to Simba in the clouds. Simba has been living in the jungle, eating bugs and singing "Hakuna Matata"—no worries, no responsibilities, no memory of who he was supposed to be. And Mufasa speaks those haunting words: *"You have forgotten who you are, and so have forgotten me ... Remember who you are."*

I think about that scene whenever I read the book of Judges.

Judges tells the story of what happened to Israel after their great leader Joshua died. Under Joshua, Israel had been thriving. They crossed the Jordan River on dry ground, watched the walls of Jericho collapse, and won victory after victory as God gave them the Promised Land. At the end of Joshua's life, the people renewed their commitment to God. Joshua gave his famous speech: "As for me and my house, we will serve the LORD." The people responded with enthusiasm: "We will serve the LORD!" It was a triumphant moment.

Then Joshua died. And just like Simba, the next generation forgot who they were.

The book of Judges opens with four words that should make your stomach drop: "After the death of Joshua ..." The great leader was gone. The generation that had witnessed God's miracles was dying off. A new generation was taking over—a generation that would slowly abandon everything their parents had taught them, everything God had done for them, everything they were supposed to be.

And just like the Pride Lands under Scar, Israel fell apart.

Judges is the story of what happens when God's people forget who they are. It's a story of compromise, disobedience, and slow spiritual drift. It's a story of a nation that had every advantage—God's presence, God's promises, God's power—and threw it all away.

But it's also a story about God's stubborn refusal to give up on his people. Even when they forgot him, he didn't forget them. Even when they abandoned him, he kept rescuing them. Even when they deserved to be destroyed, he showed mercy. Again and again, God called out to his people: *Remember who you are.*

If you've ever felt like you were drifting away from God—or watched someone you love drift away—this book has something important to say to you.

Let's dig in.

THE JOB THEY DIDN'T FINISH

When Joshua died, the conquest of Canaan wasn't completely finished. Joshua had led the Israelites in breaking the back of Canaanite resistance—winning the major battles, defeating the powerful kings, claiming the land as their own. But there were still pockets of Canaanites living throughout the territory. God had given each tribe an inheritance, a specific region that belonged to them. Now it was up to each tribe to finish the job: drive out the remaining Canaanites and fully possess their land.

This wasn't just about real estate. God had commanded Israel to completely remove the Canaanites from the land. Why? Because the Canaanites were wicked—really wicked. They worshiped false gods who demanded terrible things, including child sacrifice. They practiced every kind of evil you can imagine. God had been patient with them for centuries, but their time was up. He was using Israel as his instrument of justice, clearing the land of a corrupt civilization so his people could live there and be different—a holy nation that showed the world what it looked like to follow the true God.

God had also warned Israel what would happen if they didn't finish the job. If they let the Canaanites stick around, those Canaanites would become "thorns in your sides" and "snares" to trap them. The Israelites would be tempted to worship Canaanite gods, marry Canaanite people, and adopt Canaanite practices. Slowly but surely, they would become just like the people they were supposed to replace.

So the stakes were high. The question was: Would Israel obey?

STARTING STRONG, FADING FAST

The book of Judges opens with the Israelites doing something right. They asked God for guidance: "Who will go up first to fight against the Canaanites?" God answered clearly: "Judah shall go up. I have given the land into their hands."

Judah obeyed. They went up, and God gave them victory. They defeated a king named Adoni-Bezek (whose name means "Lord of Bezek"), captured Jerusalem, and conquered the hill country, the southern desert region, and the coastal lowlands. Caleb, the faithful spy from the wilderness generation, was still going strong. He took the city of Hebron. His nephew Othniel captured another city and won Caleb's daughter as his wife. The tribe of Simeon joined forces with Judah, and together they won more victories.

So far, so good. Judah was doing exactly what God commanded.

But then something started to change.

The narrator drops a troubling note at the end of Judah's section: "The LORD was with Judah, and they took possession of the hill country, but they could not drive out the inhabitants of the plain because they had chariots of iron."

Wait—what? God was with them, but they *couldn't* drive out the people in the plains? Iron chariots were intimidating, sure. They were the tanks of the ancient world. But since when did iron chariots stop the God who parted the Red Sea? Since when did military technology limit the power of the One who made the sun stand still?

The problem wasn't that God couldn't handle iron chariots. The problem was that Israel's faith was starting to waver. They trusted God when the odds seemed manageable, but when the enemy looked too strong, they held back.

And things only got worse from there.

THE DOWNWARD SPIRAL

After Judah's mostly-successful campaign, the narrator turns to the other tribes. And the news isn't good.

The tribe of Benjamin "did not drive out the Jebusites who lived in Jerusalem." So the Jebusites stayed.

The house of Joseph attacked Bethel and took it, but then the narrator lists failure after failure:

Manasseh "did not drive out" the inhabitants of several cities. "When Israel grew strong, they put the Canaanites to forced labor, but did not drive them out."

Ephraim "did not drive out the Canaanites who lived in Gezer." So the Canaanites lived among them.

Zebulun "did not drive out the inhabitants" of two cities. The Canaanites stayed and became forced laborers.

Asher "did not drive out" the inhabitants of multiple cities.

In fact, Asher ended up living *among* the Canaanites—the Israelites had become the minority in their own territory.

Naphtali "did not drive out" more Canaanites. Same result: the Canaanites became forced laborers but stayed in the land.

And then there's Dan. Poor Dan. The Amorites "pressed the people of Dan back into the hill country, for they did not allow them to come down to the plain." Dan didn't just fail to drive out the Canaanites—Dan got driven out by them. The tribe that was supposed to be conquering ended up being conquered.

Do you see the pattern? "Did not drive out … did not drive out … did not drive out." It's like a drumbeat of failure. And with each tribe, things got a little worse. Judah mostly succeeded. Benjamin failed a little. The northern tribes failed a lot. Dan failed completely.

This wasn't a sudden collapse. It was a slow fade. Each compromise seemed small at the time. "We'll just let them stay and make them work for us. What's the harm?" But those small compromises added up. The Canaanites who were supposed to be removed became neighbors. Then they became coworkers. Eventually, they would become family.

THE MESSENGER'S REBUKE

After this depressing catalog of failure, something dramatic happens. A messenger from the LORD goes up to a place called Bochim (which means "weepers") and delivers a stinging rebuke:

"I brought you up from Egypt and led you into the land that I swore to give to your fathers. I said, 'I will never break my covenant with you, and you shall make no covenant with the inhabitants of this land; you shall break down their altars.'

But you have not obeyed my voice. What is this you have done? So now I say, I will not drive them out before you, but they shall become thorns in your sides, and their gods shall be a snare to you."

This is God speaking through his messenger, and he's not happy. He reminds them of everything he did for them: rescuing them from slavery, bringing them into a good land, making promises he intended to keep. All he asked in return was obedience. Don't make treaties with the Canaanites. Tear down their altars. Trust me to give you victory.

But Israel didn't obey. They compromised. They made deals. They let the Canaanites stay.

And now there would be consequences. God wouldn't drive out the remaining Canaanites. They would stay in the land and become exactly what God warned they would become: thorns and snares. The people Israel refused to remove would end up being the source of their greatest troubles.

When the Israelites heard this message, they wept. That's why the place was called Bochim—"weepers." They offered sacrifices to God. It seemed like they were sorry.

But as the rest of Judges will show, their tears didn't lead to real change.

THE GENERATION THAT DIDN'T KNOW

The next section of Judges explains what went wrong on a deeper level. It's one of the saddest passages in the whole Bible: "And all that generation also were gathered to their fathers. And there arose another generation after them who did not know the LORD or the work that he had done for Israel."

Read that again. A whole generation grew up who "did not know the LORD."

How is that even possible? Their parents had seen God do incredible things. Their grandparents had walked through the Jordan River on dry ground. The stories of God's faithfulness were supposed to be passed down from generation to generation. Moses had commanded parents to teach their children about God "when you sit in your house, and when you walk by the way, and when you lie down, and when you rise."

Somehow, it didn't happen. Somehow, in the span of a single generation, the knowledge of God was lost. The children grew up, but they grew up without faith. They knew about God the way you might know about a historical figure from a textbook—distant, irrelevant, not real. They didn't *know* him.

And when you don't know God, you start looking for something else to worship.

"And the people of Israel did what was evil in the sight of the LORD and served the Baals. And they abandoned the LORD, the God of their fathers, who had brought them out of the land of Egypt. They went after other gods, from among the gods of the peoples who were around them, and bowed down to them."

The Canaanites Israel refused to drive out had now become their spiritual teachers. The gods Israel was supposed to reject became the gods Israel worshiped. The thorns and snares had done their work.

THE CYCLE THAT KEPT REPEATING

Here's where Judges gets really interesting—and really frustrating. God was angry with Israel, and rightfully so. He allowed their enemies to defeat them. Raiders plundered their land. Hostile nations oppressed them. Life became miserable.

But then something unexpected happens: "Then the LORD raised up judges, who saved them."

Wait—what? Israel rebelled against God, and God ... rescued them? They abandoned him, and he sent deliverers to save them?

Yes. That's exactly what happened. Not because Israel deserved it, but because God is compassionate. When Israel groaned under their oppression, God's heart was moved. He raised up leaders—judges—who would defeat Israel's enemies and give the people rest.

But here's the frustrating part: Israel never learned. As soon as the judge died, they went right back to worshiping other gods. In fact, the text says they "behaved worse than their fathers." Each generation sank a little lower than the one before.

This became a cycle that repeated over and over throughout the book of Judges:

1. **Israel sins** — They abandon God and worship idols.

2. **God allows oppression** — Enemies attack and oppress them.

3. **Israel cries out** — They groan under their suffering.

4. **God raises up a deliverer** — A judge rescues them.

5. **Israel has rest** — Peace for a while.

6. **The judge dies** — And Israel goes right back to sinning.

Round and round it goes. Each cycle seems to get worse. The judges become more flawed. The people become more corrupt. By the end of the book, Israel looks almost indistinguishable from the Canaanites they were supposed to replace.

THE TEST THEY FAILED

The opening section of Judges ends with a sobering summary. God left some nations in the land to "test" Israel—to see whether they would obey his commands. The test had three parts, and Israel failed all three:

First, they lived among the Canaanites. Instead of driving them out, they settled down as neighbors.

Second, they intermarried with the Canaanites. Israelite sons married Canaanite daughters. Israelite daughters married Canaanite sons. The distinct identity God had given them began to blur.

Third, they served Canaanite gods. The worship of the LORD was replaced by the worship of Baal and the other false gods of the land.

Living among. Marrying. Worshiping. Three steps, each one flowing naturally from the one before. It's not hard to see how it happened. You live next to someone long enough, you start to become friends. You become friends, your kids start dating. Your kids start dating, you start attending their religious ceremonies. Before you know it, you've become exactly what you were never supposed to be.

This is the book of Judges. It's not a story of dramatic rebellion—it's a story of slow drift. Small compromises that seemed harmless at the time. Decisions that made sense in the moment but led somewhere nobody intended to go.

WHAT THIS MEANS FOR US

So what does any of this have to do with your life? You're not an ancient Israelite. You're not trying to conquer Canaan. You've probably never even heard of Baal.

But the dangers in Judges are surprisingly relevant.

First, small compromises lead to big problems. Israel didn't abandon God overnight. They just stopped finishing what they started. They let a few Canaanites stay here, made a deal there, skipped a battle that seemed too hard. Each compromise was small. But small compromises add up. The things you tolerate in your life today will shape who you become tomorrow.

Second, faith has to be personally owned. The generation after Joshua knew *about* God, but they didn't *know* God. There's a huge difference. You can grow up in a Christian home, attend church every Sunday, memorize Bible verses, and still not have a real relationship with God. Your parents' faith won't save you. Your grandparents' faith won't save you. At some point, you have to decide for yourself: Will I follow God, or will I drift away?

Third, the people around you will influence you. Israel thought they could live among the Canaanites without becoming like them. They were wrong. The friends you choose, the content you consume, the environment you put yourself in—it all shapes you. You become like the people you spend time with. Choose wisely.

Fourth, God is patient and merciful. This might be the most amazing part of Judges. Israel failed over and over again. They deserved to be abandoned. But God kept rescuing them. Not because they earned it, but because he's compassionate. If you've drifted away from God, it's not too late. He's still ready to rescue you.

TALKING POINTS

Here are some things to think about and discuss:

1. **Israel didn't drive out the Canaanites because it seemed too hard.** What are some "hard things" God might be asking you to do that you're tempted to avoid or compromise on?

2. **A whole generation grew up "not knowing the LORD."** What do you think went wrong? How can families and churches make sure faith gets passed on to the next generation?

3. **Israel's downfall came through small compromises, not sudden rebellion.** Can you think of examples in your own life where small decisions led to bigger consequences—good or bad?

4. **The cycle in Judges shows that God keeps rescuing his people even when they don't deserve it.** Why do you think God is so patient? What does that teach us about his character?

5. **Israel became like the people they lived among.** How do your friends, your social media, and your entertainment shape who you're becoming? Are those influences pulling you toward God or away from him?

Here's something that might surprise you: God's anger and God's love aren't opposites. They're two sides of the same coin.

Think about it. If your parents didn't care about you, they wouldn't get upset when you made bad decisions. They'd just shrug and say, "Whatever, do what you want." But because they love you, they get angry when you do things that hurt yourself. Their anger proves their love.

That's what's happening in Judges. God gets angry with Israel—really angry. But his anger isn't the cold, vindictive anger of someone who wants revenge. It's the hot, passionate anger of someone who loves deeply and refuses to watch the one he loves self-destruct without doing something about it.

Even God's discipline is an act of love. When he allows Israel's enemies to oppress them, he's not abandoning them. He's trying to wake them up. He's trying to bring them back. And whenever they cry out—even when their cries are more about pain than repentance—his heart is moved, and he rescues them again.

That's the God we meet in Judges. A God who is holy enough to punish sin, but compassionate enough to keep rescuing sinners. A God who could rightfully wipe Israel off the map, but instead keeps sending deliverers to save them.

If that sounds like grace, it is. And it points forward to an even greater rescue that was still to come.

The book of Judges is not an easy read. It's full of violence, failure, and frustrating people who never seem to learn. But that's exactly why it matters. It's a mirror that shows us what happens when God's people forget who they are.

And it points us toward our desperate need for a true King—one who won't die and leave us to drift, but who will reign forever.

That King is coming. But first, we have to see just how bad things can get without him.

Turn the page. The story is about to get wild.

2

THE CYCLE BEGINS

Have you ever known someone who keeps making the same mistake over and over again?

In the movie *Finding Nemo*, Dory has short-term memory loss. She forgets things almost instantly. One minute she's terrified of the sharks, the next minute she's cheerfully swimming toward them saying, "Hi, I'm Dory!" It's played for laughs in the movie, but imagine if it wasn't funny. Imagine if forgetting things kept getting you into serious trouble—and you never learned.

That's basically the story of Israel in the book of Judges. They forget God. They get into trouble. They cry for help. God rescues them. Everything is fine for a while. Then they forget God again. More trouble. More crying. More rescue. Over and over and over again, for hundreds of years.

If you've ever read a story and wanted to yell at the characters, "Why do you keep doing that?!" then you're going to have that feeling a lot in Judges. These people never seem to learn. They have the same spiritual amnesia as Dory, except the consequences aren't funny—they're devastating.

But here's the surprising part: even though Israel keeps forgetting God, God never forgets Israel. Even though they abandon him again and again, he keeps rescuing them. Not because they deserve it. Not because they've learned their lesson. But because he's compassionate. Because he hears their cries. Because he refuses to let go of his people, even when they've let go of him.

In this chapter, we're going to meet the first three deliverers—or "judges"—that God raised up to rescue Israel. Their names are Othniel, Ehud, and Shamgar. One is a model hero. One is a sneaky left-handed assassin. And one only gets a single sentence in the whole Bible. Together, they show us something important about how God works: he saves his people in ways we never expect, using people we'd never choose.

Let's meet them.

THE PATTERN

Before we dive into the stories, we need to understand the pattern. In chapter one, we talked about the cycle that repeats throughout Judges. Now we're going to see it in action for the first time. Here's how it works:

Step 1: Israel sins. They abandon God and start worshiping the false gods of the Canaanites—gods like Baal and Asherah. These were the gods of the people Israel was supposed to drive out, but since Israel let them stay, they ended up worshiping their gods too.

Step 2: God allows oppression. Because Israel has broken their covenant with him, God "sells them" into the hands of their enemies. Foreign nations attack, conquer, and oppress Israel for years at a time.

Step 3: Israel cries out. Life under oppression is miserable. Eventually, the Israelites cry out to God for help. Now, here's something important: this crying out isn't necessarily the same as repenting. It's more like a cry of pain—"Help! This hurts!"—than a cry of true turning back to God. They want relief, but that doesn't mean they've changed their hearts.

Step 4: God raises up a deliverer. Despite Israel's half-hearted crying, God is moved by compassion. He raises up a leader—a judge—who rallies the people and defeats their enemies.

Step 5: The land has rest. Peace returns. Life gets better. The judge leads Israel, and for a while, things are okay.

Step 6: The judge dies, and Israel goes right back to sinning. And the whole cycle starts over again.

This pattern will repeat throughout the entire book of Judges. But what's really sad is that it doesn't just repeat—it spirals downward. Each time through the cycle, things get a little worse. The judges become more flawed. The people become more corrupt. The "rest" periods get shorter. It's like watching someone slowly sink in quicksand.

The first judge, Othniel, shows us the pattern in its clearest, simplest form. He's the "model" judge—the example against which all the others will be measured. And as we'll see, most of them won't measure up.

OTHNIEL: THE MODEL JUDGE

The story of Othniel is almost too simple. In fact, it's only five verses long. The narrator gives us the bare minimum—just enough to show us how the pattern works.

It starts, as it always will, with Israel's sin: "The Israelites did evil in the eyes of the LORD; they forgot the LORD their God and served the Baals and the Asherahs."

Did you catch that word? They *forgot* God. Not "rejected" or "rebelled against"—*forgot*. As if the God who rescued them from Egypt, parted the Red Sea, brought them into the Promised Land, and gave them victory after victory just … slipped their minds. How do you forget something like that?

But that's exactly what happened. And because they forgot God, they started serving other gods. The Baals were the male gods of the Canaanites, associated with storms and fertility. The Asherahs were the female goddesses, often represented by wooden poles set up at worship sites. Israel had traded the living God for blocks of wood and stone.

God's response was swift: "The anger of the LORD burned against Israel so that he sold them into the hands of Cushan-Rishathaim king of Aram Naharaim."

That's quite a name, isn't it? Cushan-Rishathaim. Say it out loud—it sounds kind of ridiculous. And that might be the point. This name is actually a mocking nickname that the Israelites gave their oppressor. It roughly means "Cushan of Double Wickedness." The Israelites couldn't throw off his yoke, but they could at least make fun of his name. Sometimes that's all oppressed people can do.

For eight long years, Israel served this foreign king. Eight years of paying tribute, of poverty, of humiliation. Finally, they couldn't take it anymore: "Then the Israelites cried out to the LORD, and he raised up for them a deliverer, Othniel son of Kenaz, Caleb's younger brother, who saved them."

We've actually met Othniel before. Back in chapter 1, he was the guy who captured the city of Debir and won Caleb's daughter as his wife. He was a proven warrior, a man of courage and faith. Now God was calling him to an even bigger task.

"The Spirit of the LORD came on him, so that he became Israel's judge and went to war." Notice where the power comes from. It's not Othniel's strength or strategy that wins the battle—it's the Spirit of God. The same God who had "sold" Israel into Cushan's hands now "gave" Cushan into Othniel's hands. God is in control of both the oppression and the deliverance. He's the Lord of history, raising up nations and bringing them down according to his purposes.

The result? "The land had peace for forty years, until Othniel son of Kenaz died." That's it. That's the whole story. No dramatic details, no clever strategies, no memorable speeches. Just the pattern, laid out simply and clearly: sin, oppression, crying out, deliverance, rest.

But here's why Othniel matters: he's the measuring stick. He's what a judge is *supposed* to look like—faithful, Spirit-empowered, victorious. As we move through the book of Judges, the judges will become more and more flawed. They'll have weird quirks, make terrible mistakes, and sometimes be barely better than the people they're saving. But Othniel? Othniel is the gold standard. Remember him, because things are about to get a lot messier.

EHUD: THE LEFT-HANDED ASSASSIN

After Othniel died, Israel did what Israel always did: "Once again the Israelites did evil in the eyes of the LORD."

This time, God gave them over to Eglon, the king of Moab. Eglon formed an alliance with the Ammonites and Amalekites, attacked Israel, and captured the "City of Palms" (that's Jericho—yes, the same city whose walls fell down for Joshua). For eighteen years, Israel served Eglon.

The narrator drops an interesting detail about Eglon: "Now Eglon was a very fat man." Why does that matter? You'll see.

Once again, Israel cried out to God. And once again, God raised up a deliverer. But this deliverer was … different. "The LORD raised up for them a deliverer—Ehud, a left-handed man, the son of Gera the Benjamite."

Left-handed. It seems like a random detail, but in that culture, it would have raised some eyebrows. Left-handedness was considered unusual, even suspicious. Left-handed warriors were specially trained—their unusual fighting style made them unpredictable in battle. Whatever the case, Ehud's left-handedness is going to be very important to the story.

Ehud had a plan. He made himself a double-edged dagger, about eighteen inches long, and strapped it to his right thigh under his clothes. Why his right thigh? Because he was left-handed. Most people are right-handed, so guards checking for weapons would look on the left side, where a right-handed person would strap a sword. Ehud's dagger was hidden where no one would think to look.

The Israelites sent Ehud to deliver their tribute payment to King Eglon—basically their taxes under Moabite occupation. Ehud presented the tribute, then started to leave with the other Israelites. But at a place called "the stone images near Gilgal," he turned back.

"I have a secret message for you, O king," Ehud said.

Eglon was intrigued. "Quiet!" he commanded, and sent all his attendants out of the room. Then he stood up from his throne to hear this secret message.

Ehud approached him. "I have a message from God for you," he said.

And then, in one swift motion, Ehud reached with his left hand, drew the dagger from his right thigh, and plunged it into Eglon's belly.

What happens next is … graphic. The Bible doesn't shy away from the details: "Even the handle sank in after the blade, and his bowels discharged. Ehud did not pull the sword out, and the fat closed in over it."

Remember how the narrator told us Eglon was very fat? Now we know why. The dagger disappeared completely into Eglon's massive belly. Ehud didn't even try to pull it out—he just left it there, locked the doors behind him, and escaped through some kind of porch or side room.

When Eglon's servants returned, they found the doors locked. They assumed their king was using the bathroom (the text literally says they thought "he was relieving himself"). So they waited. And waited. And waited some more, until it became embarrassing. Finally, they got a key and opened the doors—and found their king dead on the floor.

Meanwhile, Ehud had escaped to the hill country of Ephraim. He blew a trumpet, rallied the Israelites, and led them down to seize the crossing points of the Jordan River. When the Moabite army tried to escape back home, they were trapped. Israel struck down about ten thousand Moabite soldiers that day—all their best warriors. "That day Moab was made subject to Israel, and the land had peace for eighty years."

WHAT DO WE DO WITH THIS STORY?

Okay, let's be honest. This story is weird. It's violent. It involves deception and assassination. And it's in the Bible.

Some people get uncomfortable with stories like this. Shouldn't the Bible be … nicer? Shouldn't God's heroes be more heroic and less … stabby?

But here's the thing: the narrator isn't embarrassed by this story at all. In fact, the way it's written, with all those details about Eglon's fatness and the servants waiting awkwardly outside—it's almost funny. The original Israelite readers, who had suffered under Moabite oppression for eighteen years, would have loved this story. They would have told it around campfires, laughing at how their enemy was outsmarted by a clever left-handed warrior.

And notice what the text emphasizes: "The LORD raised up for them a deliverer." This is a story about God saving his people. Yes, the method is unexpected. Yes, Ehud uses deception and violence. But the point isn't "be like Ehud." The point is "look at how God delivers his people, even in the messiest situations."

God doesn't wait for perfect circumstances or perfect people. He meets his people in their messes and saves them anyway. That's good news for people like us, whose lives are often messier than we'd like to admit.

SHAMGAR: THE ONE-VERSE WONDER

After Ehud comes the shortest judge story in the whole book.

It's exactly one verse: "After Ehud came Shamgar son of Anath, who struck down six hundred Philistines with an oxgoad. He too saved Israel."

That's it. That's all we get.

An oxgoad was a farming tool—basically a long wooden pole with a metal point on one end for prodding oxen and a flat blade on the other end for scraping mud off plows. It could be eight feet long and pretty heavy. Not exactly a military weapon … unless you're Shamgar.

We don't know much about Shamgar. His name doesn't sound Israelite—it might be Hurrian, from a people group north of Israel. "Son of Anath" might mean he was devoted to a Canaanite goddess of war, or it might mean he came from a town called Beth-Anath. Either way, there's a good chance Shamgar wasn't even an Israelite.

And yet, "He too saved Israel."

Think about that. God used a possibly non-Israelite warrior with a farming tool to save his people from six hundred Philistine soldiers. No army. No clever plan. Just one guy with a stick.

This is what God does. He uses the unexpected. The unlikely. The people nobody would choose. He uses left-handed assassins and foreign farmers and teenaged shepherd boys with slingshots. He delights in showing his power through weakness.

The apostle Paul would later write, "God chose the foolish things of the world to shame the wise; God chose the weak things of the world to shame the strong" (1 Corinthians 1:27). Shamgar is a one-verse illustration of that truth.

WHAT THIS MEANS FOR US

So what do these three judges teach us?

First, God is patient with people who keep failing. Israel forgot God, worshiped idols, and suffered the consequences—and then did it all over again. And again. And again. Yet God kept rescuing them. His patience is astonishing. If you've ever felt like you keep making the same mistakes, keep struggling with the same sins, keep falling into the same traps—God's patience is for you too. He doesn't give up on his people.

Second, crying out to God matters, even when it's imperfect. Israel's cries weren't beautiful prayers of repentance. They were cries of pain—"Help! This hurts!" And God responded anyway. You don't have to have perfect words or perfect motives to come to God. You just have to come.

Third, God uses unexpected people and methods. A left-handed man. A foreigner with a stick. These aren't the heroes central casting would send. But God loves to work through the unexpected. Maybe you feel like you're not qualified, not talented enough, not spiritual enough for God to use. Judges says otherwise.

Fourth, even the best human deliverers aren't enough. Othniel was the ideal judge, but when he died, Israel went right back to sinning. Ehud saved Israel, but he couldn't change their hearts. Shamgar saved Israel, but we don't even know if he was one of them. Human saviors can rescue us from external enemies, but they can't free us from the enemy inside—our own stubborn, forgetful, idol-loving hearts.

For that, we need a different kind of Savior. One who doesn't just defeat our enemies but transforms our hearts. One who doesn't just give us rest for forty or eighty years but gives us rest forever.

The judges point us forward to that Savior. They show us how desperately we need him.

Fifth, God's discipline is actually a sign of his love. This might sound strange, but think about it: when God allowed Israel to be oppressed, he wasn't abandoning them—he was refusing to let them stay comfortable in their sin. A God who didn't care would have just shrugged and let Israel drift away forever. But because God loves his people, he pursues them, even through painful discipline. It's like a parent who grounds their kid—not because they hate them, but because they love them too much to let them keep making destructive choices.

The book of Hebrews puts it this way: "The Lord disciplines the one he loves" (Hebrews 12:6). When life gets hard, it doesn't always mean God is against us. Sometimes it means he loves us too much to leave us where we are.

TALKING POINTS

Here are some things to think about and discuss:

1. **Israel "forgot" God even after everything he had done for them.** Why do you think it's so easy to forget God's faithfulness? What are some ways we can help ourselves remember?

2. **The Ehud story is violent and involves deception.** Does it bother you that this is in the Bible? What do you think we're supposed to learn from stories like this?

3. **Shamgar wasn't even an Israelite, but God used him to save Israel.** What does this tell us about the kinds of people God is willing to use?

4. Israel's cycle of sin and rescue repeats over and over. Do you see any similar patterns in your own life—habits or sins you keep falling back into? What might help break the cycle?

5. The judges could save Israel from enemies but not from their own sinful hearts. Why do you think external rescue isn't enough? What kind of salvation do we really need?

The land had rest. But rest never lasts in Judges. The judges die, and the people go right back to their old ways.

There's a reason the book keeps repeating the phrase, "In those days Israel had no king." The people need more than a series of temporary deliverers. They need a permanent King.

That King is coming. But first, things are going to get a lot worse. Turn the page. The next story involves a woman with a tent peg and a really bad day for an enemy general.

3

THE WOMEN WHO WON THE WAR

In *Mulan*, everyone expects the war against the Huns to be won by soldiers—specifically, male soldiers trained in combat. That's just how things work in ancient China. Women stay home. Men fight.

But then Mulan disguises herself as a man, joins the army in her father's place, and ends up being the one who saves all of China. She outsmarts the enemy when the trained soldiers can't. She brings down an avalanche that buries the entire Hun army. And in the end, it's not the generals or the elite warriors who defeat the villain Shan Yu—it's Mulan, the girl who wasn't even supposed to be there. The movie works because it flips our expectations upside down. The person everyone underestimated turns out to be the hero.

Judges 4–5 tells a story like that—except it's not a Disney movie, and two women are involved instead of one. Israel is being crushed by a Canaanite general named Sisera, who has nine hundred iron chariots and has been oppressing them for twenty years. The Israelites need a hero. They need a mighty warrior to lead them into battle.

Instead, they get Deborah—a woman who sits under a palm tree and settles disputes. And when Deborah calls a man named Barak to lead the army, he's so unsure of himself that he refuses to go unless she comes with him. Then, when the battle is over and the enemy general is on the run, who takes him down? Not Barak. Not any of the Israelite soldiers. It's another woman—Jael, a tent-dweller who kills Sisera with a tent peg and a hammer.

This is one of the most surprising stories in the whole Bible. God wins a massive victory, but he does it through people nobody expected. The men hesitate. The women act. And in the end, everyone learns that God doesn't need mighty warriors to accomplish his purposes. He just needs people who are willing to trust him.

Let's see how it all unfolds.

THE SETUP: TWENTY YEARS OF TERROR

By now you know the pattern. Israel sins, God allows oppression, Israel cries out, God sends a deliverer. Judges 4 starts the cycle again: "Again the Israelites did evil in the eyes of the LORD, now that Ehud was dead. So the LORD sold them into the hands of Jabin king of Canaan, who reigned in Hazor."

Jabin was a Canaanite king, but the real threat was his military commander: a man named Sisera. Sisera lived in a place called Harosheth Haggoyim, and he commanded nine hundred iron chariots.

Nine hundred. Iron. Chariots.

To understand why that's terrifying, you need to know what chariots meant in the ancient world. Chariots were like the tanks of their day—mobile killing machines that could chase down infantry and cut them to pieces. They were especially devastating on flat, open ground where foot soldiers had nowhere to hide. And iron chariots were the latest military technology, far superior to anything Israel possessed.

For twenty years, Sisera used those chariots to crush Israel. Twenty years of oppression. Twenty years of fear. Twenty years of crying out to God.

Finally, God answered. But not in the way anyone expected.

DEBORAH: PROPHET, JUDGE, AND LEADER

"Now Deborah, a prophet, the wife of Lappidoth, was leading Israel at that time. She held court under the Palm of Deborah between Ramah and Bethel in the hill country of Ephraim, and the Israelites went up to her to have their disputes decided."

Let's pause here, because this is remarkable.

Deborah was a prophet—someone who spoke on God's behalf. She was also leading (or "judging") Israel, which meant people came to her for guidance and decisions. In a culture where men held almost all positions of authority, Deborah was the person everyone looked to for wisdom and direction.

The text doesn't make a big deal about this. It doesn't apologize for it or explain it away. It just states it as fact: Deborah was leading Israel. When the nation was in crisis, she was the one sitting under the palm tree, hearing from God and guiding his people. And when God was ready to rescue Israel from Sisera, he spoke through Deborah.

She sent for a man named Barak and delivered God's message: "The LORD, the God of Israel, commands you: 'Go, take with you ten thousand men of Naphtali and Zebulun and lead them up to Mount Tabor. I will lead Sisera, the commander of Jabin's army, with his chariots and his troops to the Kishon River and give him into your hands.'"

The plan was clear. God would lure Sisera and his chariots to the Kishon River, and Barak would lead the Israelite army down from Mount Tabor to attack. God promised victory: "I will give him into your hands."

Pretty straightforward, right? God gives the command. God promises to deliver the enemy. All Barak has to do is show up and fight.

Barak's response is … disappointing.

BARAK'S HESITATION

"Barak said to her, 'If you go with me, I will go; but if you don't go with me, I won't go.'" Barak wasn't willing to trust God's promise on its own. He needed Deborah to come along—maybe as a good luck charm, maybe as proof that God was really with them, maybe just because he was scared. Whatever the reason, Barak wouldn't go unless Deborah went too.

Now, to be fair, Barak does eventually go. He does gather the army. He does fight the battle. The book of Hebrews even lists him among the heroes of faith. So he's not a total coward. But compared to Deborah—who speaks for God with confidence and courage—Barak comes across as uncertain and hesitant.

Deborah agrees to go, but she adds a warning: "Certainly I will go with you. But because of the course you are taking, the honor will not be yours, for the LORD will deliver Sisera into the hands of a woman."

Barak thought he needed Deborah to win. What he didn't realize was that his hesitation would cost him the glory of the victory. God was still going to defeat Sisera—but a woman would get the credit.

At this point in the story, you'd naturally assume that woman would be Deborah. After all, she's the leader, the prophet, the one going into battle. But the narrator has a surprise in store.

THE BATTLE AT MOUNT TABOR

Barak gathered ten thousand men and marched to Mount Tabor. When Sisera heard about it, he assembled his nine hundred chariots and all his troops at the Kishon River.

This was the moment of truth. Israel's ragtag army of foot soldiers against the most advanced military technology in the region. On paper, it should have been a massacre.

But Deborah knew something Sisera didn't: God was fighting for Israel.

"Go!" Deborah told Barak. "This is the day the LORD has given Sisera into your hands. Has not the LORD gone ahead of you?"

So Barak led his men down from Mount Tabor, and something incredible happened. The text says simply: "At Barak's advance, the LORD routed Sisera and all his chariots and army by the sword."

The Lord routed them. God himself threw Sisera's army into confusion. We're not told exactly how—the poetic version in chapter 5 suggests a sudden rainstorm flooded the Kishon River and turned the battlefield into a muddy mess. Iron chariots, which were devastating on dry ground, became useless in the mud. The hunters became the hunted.

Sisera's entire army was destroyed. "All Sisera's troops fell by the sword; not a man was left."

But Sisera himself escaped. He jumped down from his chariot and fled on foot. And that's when the story takes its strangest turn.

JAEL AND THE TENT PEG

Sisera ran until he came to the tent of a woman named Jael. Her husband, Heber the Kenite, had friendly relations with King Jabin, so Sisera figured he'd be safe there. He just needed a place to hide until things blew over.

Jael came out to meet him. "Come, my lord, come right in," she said. "Don't be afraid."

Sisera went into her tent. She covered him with a blanket. He asked for water; she gave him milk. He asked her to stand at the door and tell anyone who came looking that no one was there. Then, exhausted from battle and flight, he fell asleep.

"But Jael, Heber's wife, picked up a tent peg and a hammer and went quietly to him while he lay fast asleep, exhausted. She drove the peg through his temple into the ground, and he died."

When Barak arrived, still chasing Sisera, Jael went out to meet him. "Come," she said. "I will show you the man you're looking for."

Barak went in, and there was Sisera—dead, with a tent peg through his head.

Deborah's prophecy had come true. The Lord delivered Sisera into the hands of a woman. But it wasn't the woman anyone expected.

WHAT DO WE DO WITH JAEL?

Okay, let's talk about this, because Jael's actions are … intense. She invited Sisera into her tent under the guise of hospitality. She gave him milk and covered him with a blanket. Then she killed him in his sleep. In the ancient world, hospitality was sacred—you didn't harm someone you'd welcomed into your home. Jael broke that code in the most dramatic way possible.

Is she a hero? A villain? Something in between?

The text itself doesn't give us a moral commentary. It just tells us what happened. But in chapter 5, the poetic version of this story, Deborah sings about Jael and calls her "most blessed of women." The song celebrates what Jael did, describing it in vivid detail: "She struck Sisera, she crushed his head, she shattered and pierced his temple. At her feet he sank, he fell; there he lay. At her feet he sank, he fell; where he sank, there he fell—dead."

For the Israelites who had suffered under Sisera's brutality for twenty years, Jael was a hero. She did what the soldiers couldn't do. She ended the threat. And she did it with the tools of an ordinary woman—a tent peg and a mallet, the same tools she would have used to set up her family's tent.

God doesn't always work through swords and spears. Sometimes he works through tent pegs. Sometimes he works through the people nobody expects.

THE SONG OF DEBORAH

Chapter 5 is one of the oldest pieces of poetry in the Bible—a victory song that Deborah and Barak sang after the battle. It retells the story we just read, but in a more emotional, celebratory way.

The song praises God for showing up to fight for his people: "When you, LORD, went out from Seir, when you marched from the land of Edom, the earth shook, the heavens poured, the clouds poured down water. The mountains quaked before the LORD."

This is powerful imagery. God himself marching to battle. The earth shaking. The skies opening. It's like the whole creation is responding to God's presence. When Israel couldn't win on their own, God showed up in person.

It praises the tribes who came to fight—Ephraim, Benjamin, Zebulun, Issachar, and Naphtali. These were the ones who risked their lives. Zebulun and Naphtali get special mention: they "risked their very lives on the heights of the field." They didn't hang back. They didn't calculate the odds. They showed up and fought.

But the song also shames the tribes who stayed home. And this section is devastating. Reuben had "great searchings of heart" but never actually showed up. They sat among their sheep, listening to the whistles of the shepherds, while their brothers were fighting and dying. They thought about helping. They talked about helping. They had meetings about helping. But when the moment came, they stayed with their flocks.

The tribes in Gilead stayed on the other side of the Jordan River. Dan stayed by his ships—too busy with commerce to join the fight. Asher hung out on the seacoast, probably making money from trade while the war raged inland. They all had their reasons. They all had their excuses. But in the end, they weren't there.

And then there's Meroz—a town so close to the battle that

they had no excuse not to help. The song pronounces a bitter curse on Meroz: "Curse Meroz … because they did not come to help the LORD against the mighty."

The message is clear: God's battles require his people's participation. You can't sit on the sidelines while others fight and expect to share in the victory. You can't enjoy the benefits of freedom won by someone else's sacrifice while contributing nothing yourself.

The song ends with a striking contrast. On one side is Jael, "most blessed of women," who risked everything to take down the enemy. On the other side is Sisera's mother, peering anxiously through the window, wondering why her son hasn't come home yet. Her attendants reassure her: "He's probably just dividing the plunder."

The irony is brutal. While Sisera's mother imagines her son enjoying the spoils of victory, he's already dead—killed by a woman with a tent peg. The mighty warrior who terrorized Israel for twenty years didn't die in glorious battle. He died hiding in a tent, defeated by someone he never saw coming.

The final verse of the song is a prayer: "So may all your enemies perish, LORD! But may all who love you be like the sun when it rises in its strength."

It's a prayer for God's kingdom to come. A prayer that all who oppose God would fall, and all who love him would shine. In the context of Judges, it's also a challenge to Israel: Which side are you on? Are you an enemy of God, chasing after other gods? Or do you love him—really love him—and show that love through faithful obedience?

WHAT THIS MEANS FOR US

So what does this wild story teach us?

First, God uses unexpected people. Deborah was a woman in a world that expected male leaders. Jael was a tent-dwelling nomad with no military training. Neither of them fits the profile of a mighty warrior. But God used them both to accomplish something the "qualified" people couldn't do. If you've ever felt like you're not the right person for the job—not talented enough, not experienced enough, not the "type" God usually uses—this story says otherwise.

Second, hesitation has consequences. Barak's refusal to go without Deborah cost him the honor of the victory. He still went, and that's good. But because he hesitated when God gave a clear command, he missed out on something he could have had. When God calls us to act, delay and doubt have a price.

Third, God's battles require our participation. The tribes who stayed home didn't get cursed because God needed their military help. He won the battle just fine without them. They got cursed because they refused to participate in what God was doing. Being part of God's people means showing up, not sitting on the sidelines.

Fourth, victory belongs to God. At the end of the day, it wasn't Deborah's wisdom or Barak's army or Jael's tent peg that won the battle. It was God. He routed the enemy. He flooded the river. He delivered Sisera into Israel's hands. The human participants played their parts, but the victory was his. The song makes this clear: "So may all your enemies perish, LORD!"

Fifth, the story isn't over. The chapter ends with a hopeful note: "Then the land had peace forty years." But by now, we know that peace in Judges never lasts. The cycle will start again. Israel will forget God again. And another crisis will come. The book is pointing us toward our need for something more permanent—a King who will break the cycle forever.

TALKING POINTS

Here are some things to think about and discuss:

1. **Deborah was a woman leading Israel in a male-dominated culture.** What does her story teach us about the kinds of people God uses? Are there ways we limit who we think God can work through?

2. **Barak wouldn't go to battle without Deborah.** Was his request reasonable, or was it a failure of faith? What's the difference between wanting support and refusing to trust God's promise?

3. **Some tribes fought while others stayed home.** What excuses do people today use to avoid participating in what God is doing? How can we avoid being like Reuben or Dan or Meroz?

4. **Jael's actions were violent and involved deception.** How do you make sense of this story? What do you think we're supposed to learn from it?

5. **The song celebrates God's victory, not human achievement.** How can we make sure we give God credit for the good things that happen in our lives instead of taking the credit ourselves?

The land had peace for forty years. The iron chariots were destroyed. The mighty general lay dead in a tent, defeated by a woman with a hammer.

God had won again. And he had done it in a way that left no doubt about who deserved the credit. It wasn't the professional soldiers. It wasn't the mighty warriors. It was a prophetess under a palm tree and a tent-dweller with a mallet. God took the "weak things of the world to shame the strong," as the apostle Paul would later write.

But the real question remained: Would Israel remember him this time? Would they learn from this incredible deliverance and stay faithful? Or would they forget—again—and go chasing after the same old false gods that had gotten them into trouble in the first place?

You already know the answer. Turn the page.

4

THE RELUCTANT HERO AND THE BRAMBLE KING

In *How to Train Your Dragon*, Hiccup is not exactly Viking material. He's scrawny. He's awkward. He's terrible at all the things Vikings are supposed to be good at—fighting, hunting, being tough. When everyone else charges into battle against dragons, Hiccup gets in the way and makes things worse. His own father, the chief, is embarrassed by him. The other teenagers mock him. Hiccup himself is convinced he'll never measure up.

But here's the twist: Hiccup ends up being the one who changes everything. Not by becoming a mighty warrior, but by using his apparent weaknesses—his curiosity, his gentleness, his refusal to do things the "normal" way—to befriend a dragon instead of killing one. In the end, the village's most unlikely hero becomes its greatest one.

The story works because it flips the script on what a hero looks like. The person everyone counted out turns out to be exactly who they needed.

Judges 6–9 tells a story like that—at least at first. Gideon is hiding in a winepress, terrified of the enemy, when God calls him a "mighty warrior." He argues with God, tests God, doubts God at almost every turn. He's about as far from a confident hero as you can get.

But God uses him anyway. In fact, God goes out of his way to make sure Israel's army is as small and weak as possible before the battle, just so everyone will know that the victory belongs to God, not to human strength.

It's an incredible story of God's power working through human weakness.

But then things take a dark turn. After the victory, Gideon starts making bad decisions. His family falls apart. His son Abimelech becomes one of the most brutal villains in the entire Bible. What started as a story of unlikely triumph ends in tragedy and civil war.

This is a complicated chapter. It has soaring highs and devastating lows. But it teaches us something crucial: God can use weak people to do amazing things—but even people God uses can fall, and their failures have consequences.

Let's meet Gideon.

HIDING IN A WINEPRESS

The cycle begins the same way it always does: "The Israelites did evil in the eyes of the LORD, and for seven years he gave them into the hands of the Midianites."

This time the oppression was brutal. Every year, just when the Israelites planted their crops, the Midianites would sweep in from the east like a swarm of locusts. They'd bring their livestock, let them graze on Israel's fields, and take everything—grain, sheep, cattle, donkeys. Year after year. The Israelites were so desperate they started living in caves and mountain hideouts just to survive.

Finally, they cried out to God.

God's first response was surprising. He didn't immediately send a deliverer. Instead, he sent a prophet who reminded Israel why they were in this mess: "I brought you out of Egypt. I gave you this land. I told you not to worship the gods of the Amorites. But you have not listened to me."

God wanted Israel to understand their situation before he rescued them from it. Sometimes God cares more about our understanding than our comfort.

Then something unexpected happened. The Angel of the Lord showed up and sat down under an oak tree in a town called Ophrah. Nearby, a man named Gideon was threshing wheat—but not on a threshing floor, where you'd normally do it. He was hiding in a winepress, trying to keep his grain hidden from the Midianites.

Picture that for a second. Threshing wheat means tossing it into the air so the wind can blow away the chaff. But Gideon was doing this down in a pit, where there was no wind, because he was too scared to work out in the open. This is not exactly a portrait of courage.

And yet, the Angel of the Lord greeted him with these words: "The LORD is with you, mighty warrior."

Mighty warrior? Gideon must have looked around to see if someone else was standing there. He didn't feel like a mighty warrior. He felt like a terrified farmer trying not to starve.

GIDEON'S DOUBTS

Gideon's response was basically, "If the LORD is with us, why has all this happened? Where are all the miracles our ancestors told us about? It feels like God has abandoned us."

It's an honest question. Maybe you've asked something like it yourself. If God is real, why is life so hard? If God loves us, why does he let bad things happen?

God didn't answer Gideon's theological questions. Instead, he gave him a mission: "Go in the strength you have and save Israel out of Midian's hand. Am I not sending you?"

Gideon protested. "But Lord, how can I save Israel? My clan is the weakest in our tribe. And I'm the youngest in my family." Translation: I'm a nobody. You've got the wrong guy.

God's answer was simple and profound: "I will be with you."

That's it. Not "Don't worry, you're stronger than you think." Not "Here's a detailed battle plan." Just: "I will be with you." That promise—God's presence—is supposed to be enough. It's the same promise God gave to Moses, to Joshua, to countless others. Everything you need is contained in those five words.

But Gideon wasn't convinced. He asked for a sign. Then another sign. Then another. He prepared an offering, and the Angel of the Lord touched it with his staff, causing fire to consume it. Gideon was terrified—he realized he'd been talking to God himself.

That night, God told Gideon to tear down his father's altar to Baal and cut down the Asherah pole beside it. Gideon obeyed—but he did it at night, because he was afraid of his family and the townspeople.

Do you see the pattern? Gideon believes enough to obey, but he's scared the whole time. He's not a fearless hero. He's a frightened man taking one shaky step after another.

And honestly? That's probably more relatable than a superhero who never doubts.

THE FLEECE

Even after all this, Gideon still needed more assurance. You've probably heard the famous story of Gideon's fleece.

Gideon said to God, "If you're really going to save Israel through me, give me a sign. I'll put a wool fleece on the threshing floor tonight. If there's dew only on the fleece and the ground is dry, then I'll know you'll save Israel through me."

The next morning, the fleece was soaking wet and the ground was dry. Gideon wrung out enough water to fill a bowl.

But Gideon still wasn't satisfied. "Don't be angry with me," he said, "but let me make one more test. This time let the fleece be dry and the ground covered with dew."

God did it. The next morning, the fleece was dry and the ground was wet.

Now, before you think this is a great model for decision-making ("I'll just put out a fleece and see what God does!"), notice something important: Gideon was testing God because he lacked faith. God was incredibly patient with him, but Gideon's fleece-testing wasn't a sign of spiritual maturity. It was a sign of how much he struggled to trust.

The amazing thing is that God worked with Gideon anyway. God doesn't wait until we have perfect faith to use us. He meets us where we are—doubts and all—and gently leads us forward.

THREE HUNDRED MEN

Gideon gathered an army. Thirty-two thousand men showed up to fight the Midianites.

Then God said something shocking: "You have too many men." Too many? The Midianites and their allies were spread across the valley "thick as locusts," with camels "as numerous as sand on the seashore." And God thought Israel had too many soldiers?

Here's God's reasoning: "If I let Israel win with this many men, they'll brag that they did it themselves. They'll say, 'My own strength saved me.' I can't let that happen."

So God told Gideon to send home anyone who was afraid. Twenty-two thousand men left. Only ten thousand remained.

Still too many. God had Gideon take the remaining men down to a stream to drink. Those who knelt down to drink were sent home. Those who lapped water from their hands—three hundred men—stayed.

Why the lapping test? The text doesn't tell us these men were more vigilant or spiritually superior. The point isn't that the three hundred were special. The point is that God reduced the army to almost nothing so that everyone would know the victory came from him.

Three hundred men against an army too numerous to count. Humanly speaking, it was impossible. But that's exactly where God wanted them.

TORCHES, JARS, AND TRUMPETS

The battle plan was bizarre. Gideon divided his three hundred men into three groups. Each man got a trumpet and a clay jar with a torch hidden inside. In the middle of the night, they surrounded the Midianite camp.

At Gideon's signal, they all blew their trumpets, smashed their jars, held up their torches, and shouted, "A sword for the LORD and for Gideon!"

That's it. No swords. No charge. Just noise, fire, and confusion.

And it worked. The Midianites panicked. In the darkness and chaos, they started attacking each other. The entire army fled in terror, and Israel's three hundred men hadn't even drawn a weapon.

The victory was total. The Midianite threat was broken. And everyone knew it wasn't because Israel had a superior army. It was because God fought for them.

This is the high point of the Gideon story. God took a terrified man hiding in a winepress and used him to deliver an entire nation. God took an army of three hundred and defeated an enemy that seemed invincible. God's power was displayed most clearly through human weakness.

If the story ended here, it would be one of the most inspiring accounts in the Bible.

But the story doesn't end here.

THE BEGINNING OF THE FALL

After the victory, things started to go wrong.

The tribe of Ephraim was angry that Gideon hadn't called them to fight from the beginning. Gideon smoothed things over with a diplomatic answer. But then Gideon asked the towns of Succoth and Penuel for food for his exhausted troops, and they refused to help. They were hedging their bets—what if Gideon lost? They didn't want to be caught supporting him.

Gideon was furious. He promised to punish them when he returned. And he did—brutally. The leaders of Succoth were beaten with thorns and briars. The tower of Penuel was torn down, and its men were killed.

Then the Israelites made Gideon an offer: "Rule over us—you, your son, and your grandson—because you saved us from Midian."

Gideon's answer sounded humble: "I will not rule over you, nor will my son. The LORD will rule over you."

Good answer, right? But watch what Gideon did next.

He collected gold earrings from the plunder—a huge amount, over forty pounds of gold—and made them into an "ephod." An ephod was a priestly garment used to seek God's guidance. But Gideon wasn't a priest, and the ephod was supposed to be at the tabernacle, not in Gideon's hometown.

By making this ephod, Gideon set himself up as an alternative spiritual authority. And the results were disastrous: "All the Israelites were unfaithful to God and worshiped it, so it became a trap for Gideon and his family."

Gideon refused the title of king but started acting like one. He had many wives and seventy sons. He even named one of his sons "Abimelech"—which means "My father is king."

His words said one thing. His actions said another. And after he died, everything fell apart.

ABIMELECH: THE BRAMBLE KING

After Gideon's death, one of his sons decided he wanted

power—not shared with seventy brothers, but all for himself.

Abimelech went to his mother's relatives in Shechem and convinced them to support his bid for leadership. "Isn't it better to have one ruler than seventy?" he argued. They agreed and gave him money from the temple of their god, Baal-Berith.

With that money, Abimelech hired a gang of thugs. Then he went to his father's house in Ophrah and murdered his seventy brothers—all of them on a single stone. It was a massacre. Only the youngest brother, Jotham, escaped by hiding.

The people of Shechem crowned Abimelech king. It was Israel's first attempt at monarchy—and it was soaked in blood.

But Jotham wasn't done. He climbed a nearby mountain and shouted a story—a fable that would expose exactly what Shechem had done.

THE FABLE OF THE TREES

"Once upon a time," Jotham called out, "the trees went looking for a king."

They asked the olive tree: "Come rule over us." But the olive tree refused. "Should I give up my oil, which honors gods and humans, just to hold sway over trees?"

They asked the fig tree: "Come rule over us." The fig tree refused too. "Should I give up my sweet fruit just to hold sway over trees?"

They asked the vine: "Come rule over us." Same answer. "Should I give up my wine, which cheers gods and humans, just to hold sway over trees?"

Finally, the trees asked the thornbush—the bramble, the most useless plant in the forest. And the bramble said yes. "If you really want to anoint me king, come take shelter in my shade. But if not, let fire come out of me and consume the cedars of Lebanon!"

The message was clear. The olive, fig, and vine—the useful, productive, honorable trees—had no interest in ruling. Only the worthless bramble wanted power. And what can a bramble offer? No fruit, no oil, no shade. Just thorns and fire.

Abimelech was the bramble. Shechem had rejected good leadership and chosen a worthless, dangerous man. And Jotham pronounced a curse: fire would come from Abimelech to consume Shechem, and fire would come from Shechem to consume Abimelech.

Then Jotham fled for his life.

FIRE CONSUMES FIRE

For three years Abimelech ruled. Then God sent a spirit of hostility between Abimelech and Shechem. The very people who had made him king turned against him.

What followed was brutal civil war. Abimelech crushed a rebellion in Shechem, killing everyone in the city. He burned a thousand people alive when they took refuge in a temple tower. Then he attacked another city called Thebez.

But at Thebez, Abimelech's violence finally caught up with him. As he approached a tower to set it on fire, a woman dropped a millstone from the top—and it crushed his skull.

Mortally wounded, Abimelech ordered his armor-bearer to kill him with a sword. He didn't want people to say a woman had killed him. But it didn't matter. Everyone knew.

Jotham's curse had come true. Fire from Abimelech had

consumed Shechem. Fire from Shechem—in the form of a woman with a millstone—had consumed Abimelech.

The narrator makes sure we don't miss the point: "Thus God repaid the wickedness that Abimelech had done to his father by murdering his seventy brothers."

Evil destroyed evil. The bramble king was gone.

WHAT THIS MEANS FOR US

This is a heavy chapter. What do we take away from it?

First, God uses weak and fearful people. Gideon was hiding in a winepress. He argued with God. He tested God repeatedly. He was scared at almost every step. And God used him anyway. Your weakness is not a disqualification—it might be exactly where God wants to display his power.

Second, God gets the glory for the victory. The army was reduced to three hundred men precisely so Israel couldn't brag about their own strength. When God works through our weakness, it becomes obvious that he's the one doing it. That's the point.

Third, even people God uses can make terrible mistakes. Gideon's ephod led Israel into idolatry. His many wives and his son Abimelech brought disaster. Being used by God once doesn't guarantee faithfulness forever. We need to stay humble and vigilant to the end.

Fourth, bad leadership has devastating consequences. The bramble king brought nothing but destruction. Choosing leaders based on ambition, charisma, or family connection rather than character and godliness leads to disaster—in nations, in churches, and in our own lives.

Fifth, God brings justice in the end. Abimelech's violence came back on his own head. Shechem's treachery was repaid. God is patient, but he is also just. Evil may seem to win for a while, but it doesn't last.

TALKING POINTS

1. **Gideon was terrified and full of doubts, yet God called him a "mighty warrior."** What does this tell us about how God sees us versus how we see ourselves?

2. **God reduced Gideon's army so Israel couldn't take credit for the victory.** Why do you think it's so important to God that he gets the glory? What happens when we start taking credit for things God has done?

3. **Gideon refused the title of king but started acting like one.** Why is it dangerous when our words and actions don't match? Can you think of examples of this in your own life?

4. **Jotham's fable shows that worthless people often seek power while capable people don't.** What should we look for when choosing leaders—in school, church, or anywhere else?

5. **Abimelech's violence eventually came back on his own head.** How does this story show that evil destroys itself? Does knowing that God brings justice help you when you see injustice in the world?

The land had rest for forty years while Gideon lived. But after his death, Israel immediately returned to worshiping Baal. They forgot God. They forgot Gideon. And they got exactly the kind of leader they deserved—a bramble king who burned everything he touched.

The downward spiral continues. And as we'll see, the judges who come next are even more flawed than Gideon. Turn the page.

5

THE OUTCAST AND THE TERRIBLE PROMISE

Have you ever felt like you didn't belong?

In the movie *Coco*, Miguel comes from a family that has banned music for generations. He loves music more than anything, but he's told he can never pursue it because of something that happened long before he was born. He's caught between who his family says he should be and who he feels he really is. He doesn't fit.

Or think about kids at school who get excluded because of their family situation—maybe their parents are divorced, or they live with a grandparent, or they come from a different background than everyone else. They didn't choose their circumstances. They just got dealt a hard hand, and other people treat them differently because of it.

Judges 11 introduces us to a man named Jephthah who knew exactly what that felt like.

Jephthah was born to a prostitute. His father, Gilead, had other sons by his legitimate wife, and when those sons grew up, they kicked Jephthah out of the family. "You're not getting any of our inheritance," they said. "You are the son of another woman." Jephthah fled and became the leader of a gang of out-laws—"worthless fellows," the Bible calls them.

He was rejected. An outcast. A nobody.

But when trouble came to Israel—when the Ammonites threatened to destroy them—guess who the leaders of Gilead came crawling to for help? The very man they had thrown away.

This is one of the strangest and saddest stories in the book of Judges. It has moments of triumph and moments of tragedy. It shows us a flawed hero who wins a great victory but makes a terrible vow that costs him everything. It shows us what happens when people try to bargain with God. And it shows us that even when God uses someone, that doesn't mean everything they do is wise or right.

Let's dive in.

ROCK BOTTOM

Before we meet Jephthah, we need to see just how bad things have gotten in Israel.

Judges 10:6 doesn't just say Israel sinned again. It piles up the sins like a stack of bricks: "The Israelites did evil in the eyes of the LORD. They served the Baals and the Ashtoreths, and the gods of Aram, the gods of Sidon, the gods of Moab, the gods of the Ammonites and the gods of the Philistines."

Did you catch that? Seven different pagan religions. Israel wasn't just dabbling in idolatry anymore—they had gone all in. They were worshiping every god in the region except the one true God who had rescued them from Egypt.

"Because the Israelites forsook the LORD and no longer served him, he became angry with them." God handed them over to two enemies at once: the Philistines in the west and the Ammonites in the east. For eighteen years, the Ammonites "shattered and crushed" the Israelites in the region of Gilead (that's the area east of the Jordan River). Eventually, they even crossed the Jordan and started attacking Judah, Benjamin, and Ephraim.

Israel was desperate. So they did what they always did— they cried out to God.

But this time, something different happened.

GOD SAYS NO

"We have sinned against you," the Israelites confessed, "forsaking our God and serving the Baals."

It sounds like repentance, right? But God wasn't buying it.

"When the Egyptians, the Amorites, the Ammonites, the Philistines, the Sidonians, the Amalekites and the Maonites oppressed you and you cried to me for help, did I not save you from their hands? But you have forsaken me and served other gods, so I will no longer save you. Go and cry out to the gods you have chosen. Let them save you when you are in trouble!"

Whoa.

God basically said, "You've used me like a vending machine—drop in a prayer when you're in trouble, get your rescue, then go right back to worshiping other gods. I'm done. You chose those gods—let them help you."

This is one of the most terrifying moments in the book of Judges. For the first time, God threatens to abandon his people completely. He's not just disciplining them; he's warning them that they're on the edge of losing everything.

Israel's response? They didn't argue or make excuses. They said, "We have sinned. Do with us whatever you think best, but please rescue us now." And then—here's the key—they actually did something about it. "They got rid of the foreign gods among them and served the LORD."

What happened next reveals something incredible about God's heart: "He could bear Israel's misery no longer."

Even though Israel deserved to be abandoned, even though their repentance might have been more about escaping pain than truly loving God, the Lord couldn't stand to watch his people suffer. His compassion overcame his anger.

That's not weakness. That's love. God is both holy enough to demand justice and compassionate enough to show mercy—and somehow, miraculously, both of those things exist in him at the same time.

This passage shows us something crucial about God's character. He's not a pushover who can be manipulated. When Israel treated him like a vending machine—insert prayer, receive deliverance, go back to idols—he called them out on it. He has standards. He expects faithfulness. He won't be used.

But he's also not a cold, distant judge waiting to condemn. When he saw his people suffering—even people who had brought the suffering on themselves—his heart broke. He "could bear Israel's misery no longer." The God of the Bible feels. He grieves over our pain. He longs for our return.

Both things are true: God takes sin seriously, and God loves us more than we can imagine. Understanding both sides of his character helps us understand the whole Bible.

THE OUTCAST RETURNS

The Ammonites gathered for war. The Israelites assembled to meet them. But there was a problem: nobody wanted to lead.

The elders of Gilead asked each other, "Who will lead the attack against the Ammonites? Whoever he is will be head over all who live in Gilead."

Enter Jephthah.

The text introduces him bluntly: "Jephthah the Gileadite was a mighty warrior. His father was Gilead; his mother was a prostitute."

There it is. Jephthah's whole life was defined by that one fact. He was skilled and strong—a "mighty warrior"—but none of that mattered to his half-brothers. They drove him out of the family because of who his mother was.

So Jephthah fled to a place called Tob, where he gathered a group of "worthless fellows" around him. Think of him like Robin Hood—an outlaw leader, probably raiding and surviving on the margins of society.

But now the very people who had rejected him needed him. The elders of Gilead traveled to Tob and made Jephthah an offer: "Come, be our commander, so we can fight the Ammonites."

Jephthah's response was bitter: "Didn't you hate me and drive me from my father's house? Why do you come to me now, when you're in trouble?" You can almost hear the hurt in his voice. Where were you when I needed you? Now that *you* need *me*, suddenly I'm good enough?

But the elders were desperate. They promised that if Jephthah led them to victory, he would become the permanent leader—the "head"—over all of Gilead.

Jephthah agreed. The outcast became the commander. The rejected one became the leader.

THE NEGOTIATOR

Before fighting, Jephthah tried diplomacy. He sent messengers to the king of Ammon asking, "What do you have against us?"

The Ammonite king claimed that Israel had stolen his land when they came out of Egypt three hundred years earlier. He demanded it back.

Jephthah's response shows he knew his history. He sent a detailed message explaining that Israel hadn't taken Ammonite land—they had taken land from the Amorite king Sihon, who had attacked them first. Israel had been living in that territory for three hundred years. If the Ammonite god Chemosh had given the Ammonites their land, why would they complain about what Israel's God had given Israel?

It was a solid argument. But the king of Ammon ignored it.

So war became inevitable.

THE TERRIBLE VOW

Here's where the story takes a dark turn. "Then the Spirit of the LORD came on Jephthah." This should be good news—God is empowering his chosen deliverer, just like he did with Othniel and Gideon. Jephthah gathered his forces and prepared to attack.

But then Jephthah did something unnecessary. Something that would haunt him forever.

"Jephthah made a vow to the LORD: 'If you give the Ammonites into my hands, whatever comes out of the door of my house to meet me when I return in triumph from the

Ammonites will be the LORD's, and I will sacrifice it as a burnt offering.'"

Stop and think about that vow. When someone returned home victorious in the ancient world, who came out to greet them? Not the family goat. People came out. Family members came out. Jephthah almost certainly knew he was vowing a human sacrifice.

Why would he do this? Maybe he didn't fully trust God's Spirit to be enough. Maybe his rough background in pagan-influenced territory had warped his understanding of what God wanted. Maybe he thought he could bargain with God—give God something valuable to guarantee victory.

Whatever his reasoning, it was terribly wrong. God had already given Jephthah his Spirit. God had already chosen him as deliverer. Jephthah didn't need to bargain. He didn't need to make deals. He just needed to trust.

But he didn't.

VICTORY AND DEVASTATION

Jephthah attacked the Ammonites, and God gave him a crushing victory. He destroyed twenty towns and devastated the Ammonite army. The threat was over.

"When Jephthah returned to his home in Mizpah, who should come out to meet him but his daughter, dancing to the sound of timbrels!"

His daughter. His only child. The text says simply: "She was an only child. Except for her he had neither son nor daughter."

Can you imagine the horror of that moment? Jephthah had won everything—and lost everything. The victory that should have been the greatest moment of his life became the worst.

"When he saw her, he tore his clothes and cried, 'Oh no, my daughter! You have brought me down and I am devastated. I have made a vow to the LORD that I cannot break.'"

Notice something troubling: Jephthah blames his daughter. "You have brought me down." But she hadn't done anything wrong. She was just doing what any daughter would do—running out to celebrate her father's victory. The fault was entirely his.

His daughter's response is heartbreaking: "My father, you have given your word to the LORD. Do to me just as you promised, now that the LORD has avenged you of your enemies, the Ammonites." She only asked for two months to go into the hills with her friends and weep, because she would never marry or have children.

When she returned, Jephthah "did to her as he had vowed."

The text doesn't elaborate. It doesn't need to. A father's foolish vow cost his only daughter her life.

WHAT ARE WE SUPPOSED TO THINK?

This is one of the hardest stories in the Bible. A few things we should notice:

The Bible reports it; it doesn't approve it. Just because something is recorded in Scripture doesn't mean God endorsed it. The narrator never says Jephthah was right to make this vow or to carry it out. In fact, the whole story is framed as a tragedy— Israel won the battle, but the victory is overshadowed by grief.

Human sacrifice was forbidden in Israel's law. Leviticus 18 and Deuteronomy 12 and 18 all explicitly prohibit child sacrifice. Jephthah should have known better. The fact that he went through with it shows how far Israel had drifted from truly knowing God's ways.

God never asked for this. Jephthah's vow came from Jephthah, not from God. God gave Jephthah his Spirit before the vow was ever made. The vow wasn't faith—it was an attempt to manipulate or bargain with God, and it backfired horribly.

Even heroes in the Bible are deeply flawed. The book of Hebrews lists Jephthah among the heroes of faith. That doesn't mean everything he did was right. It means God can use broken people—and Jephthah was very, very broken.

MORE TRAGEDY: CIVIL WAR

As if Jephthah's personal tragedy wasn't enough, the story continues with more violence—this time between Israelites.

The tribe of Ephraim was furious that Jephthah hadn't invited them to fight the Ammonites. "We're going to burn down your house with you in it!" they threatened.

Sound familiar? Ephraim had made the same complaint to Gideon years earlier. Gideon defused the situation with a humble, diplomatic answer.

Jephthah wasn't Gideon. He didn't do diplomacy. He gathered his troops and attacked Ephraim.

The Gileadites captured the crossing points of the Jordan River. When fleeing Ephraimites tried to cross, the Gileadites would ask them to say "Shibboleth." Because of their regional accent, Ephraimites pronounced it "Sibboleth"—and that one mispronunciation got them killed.

Forty-two thousand Ephraimites died in this civil war.

Israelites killing Israelites. Brothers slaughtering brothers.

The victory over Ammon was supposed to bring peace. Instead, it brought grief, death, and division. The deliverer who started as an outcast ended up presiding over tragedy after tragedy.

THE MINOR JUDGES

The chapter closes with brief notices about three more judges: Ibzan, Elon, and Abdon. We know almost nothing about them—just where they came from, how many children they had, how long they judged, and where they were buried.

Ibzan of Bethlehem had thirty sons and thirty daughters. He arranged marriages for all of them, expanding his influence through family alliances. He judged for seven years.

Elon the Zebulunite judged for ten years. That's literally all we know about him.

Abdon had forty sons and thirty grandsons, all of whom rode on donkeys—a sign of prosperity and peace. He judged for eight years.

But the contrast with Jephthah is striking. Jephthah had one child and lost her. Ibzan had sixty children and saw them all married. Abdon had seventy descendants riding around on donkeys, enjoying the good life.

Why does the writer put these details side by side? Perhaps to show us how different things could have been. Perhaps to highlight that God distributes his blessings differently, and we don't always understand why. Perhaps simply to remind us that between the dramatic stories of conflict, there were quieter periods of peace and stability—times when donkeys carried prosperous families instead of warriors rushing to battle.

There's also something important in those repeated death notices: "Then Ibzan died … Then Elon died … Then Abdon died." Human saviors come and go. They rise, they serve, they die. No matter how successful or peaceful their reign, it ends. The people of Israel needed more than a series of temporary leaders who kept dying. They needed a king who would reign forever.

Life in Israel went on. Judges rose and fell. The people continued their cycle of forgetting and remembering. But the careful reader starts to notice something: after Gideon, the narrator never again says "the land had rest." Something has been lost. The peace that earlier judges brought—real, God-given rest—seems to have faded. Now there's just a succession of leaders, one after another, trying to hold things together.

The spiral continues downward.

WHAT THIS MEANS FOR US

First, God uses broken people—but that doesn't make everything they do right. Jephthah was a mighty warrior used by God. He was also a man whose foolish vow led to unspeakable tragedy. Being used by God doesn't mean we're perfect or that our judgment is always sound.

Second, we can't bargain with God. Jephthah tried to make a deal—"If you do this, I'll give you that." But God isn't a negotiating partner waiting for us to offer a good enough price. He gives us his Spirit freely. He calls us to trust him, not to manipulate him.

Third, our words matter. "I have made a vow to the LORD that I cannot break," Jephthah said. Rash promises have consequences. The Bible warns us to be careful about what we vow, because we'll be held to it.

Fourth, rejection and bitterness can shape us in dangerous ways. Jephthah's harsh upbringing left marks on his character. His bitterness toward Ephraim led to civil war. The wounds we carry—if we don't let God heal them—can lead us to wound others.

Fifth, even in the darkest stories, God is working. Israel was delivered from the Ammonites. The immediate crisis was resolved. But the deliverance came with such a heavy cost that we're left longing for a better savior—one who doesn't make foolish vows, who doesn't need to bargain with God, who brings peace instead of more bloodshed.

TALKING POINTS

1. **God threatened to stop saving Israel.** What finally moved him to help anyway? What does this tell us about God's character?

2. **Jephthah was rejected by his family but became their deliverer.** Can you think of other stories—in the Bible or elsewhere—where someone rejected becomes someone essential?

3. **Why do you think Jephthah made his vow?** What was he trying to accomplish? What does this reveal about his understanding of God?

4. **The civil war with Ephraim killed 42,000 Israelites.** Compare how Gideon handled Ephraim's complaint (Judges 8:1–3) with how Jephthah handled it. What can we learn about conflict resolution?

5. **The minor judges (Ibzan, Elon, Abdon) barely get

mentioned. What might their brief, peaceful reigns teach us about faithfulness in "ordinary" times?

Jephthah judged Israel for six years. Then he died.

The cycle continues. Israel's saviors are becoming more flawed, more broken, more tragic. The victories are tainted with sorrow. The peace never lasts.

One more judge remains—the strongest and the weakest, the most spectacular and the most self-destructive of them all.

His name is Samson. Turn the page.

6

THE STRONGEST AND THE WEAKEST

In Disney's *Hercules*, the son of Zeus is born with incredible strength. He can lift boulders, fight monsters, and defeat any enemy. But here's the thing about Hercules—he's kind of a mess. He knocks over buildings by accident. He doesn't fit in anywhere. And even though he has all this power, he keeps making choices that get him into trouble. He wants to be a hero, but he doesn't really understand what that means.

There's a scene where the villain, Hades, takes away Hercules's strength. Suddenly, this unstoppable hero is just a regular guy—weak, helpless, chained up and about to watch everything he loves get destroyed. It's only when he's willing to sacrifice himself for someone else that he finally becomes the hero he was born to be.

The story of Samson in Judges 13–16 starts out looking like it might be that kind of story. A miraculous birth. Incredible strength. A destiny to save his people. All the ingredients for a classic hero's journey.

But Samson never becomes that hero. Not really.

Samson is the strongest man who ever lived—and somehow

also the weakest. He could rip a lion apart with his bare hands but couldn't resist a pretty face. He could defeat entire armies but couldn't conquer his own selfishness. He had more potential than any judge before him and wasted almost all of it.

This is the most frustrating, most tragic, and most important story in the book of Judges. It's frustrating because Samson keeps making the same terrible choices. It's tragic because we watch someone with every advantage throw it all away. And it's important because Samson isn't just one man—he's a mirror of Israel herself. Everything wrong with Israel is concentrated in this one larger-than-life character.

By the end of this story, you might want to throw the book across the room. But stick with it. Because even in the middle of this disaster, God is still working. And there's something here we desperately need to see.

A SILENT CRY

The cycle begins the same way it always does: "Again the Israelites did evil in the eyes of the LORD, and he gave them into the hands of the Philistines for forty years."

Forty years. That's twice as long as any previous oppression. The Philistines weren't just raiders who showed up occasionally—they were occupiers who settled in and took over. They controlled the coastal region, had superior iron technology, and dominated Israel economically and militarily.

But here's what's really disturbing: there's no cry for help.

Go back and read the previous stories. When Israel was oppressed, they "cried out to the LORD." Their cry wasn't perfect repentance, but at least they knew they were in trouble. At least they wanted to be rescued.

Not this time. In the Samson story, Israel never cries out. They've become so comfortable with Philistine rule that they don't even want to be saved anymore. Later in the story, when Samson starts fighting Philistines, his own people—men from the tribe of Judah—will come to arrest him. Their complaint? "Don't you realize the Philistines are rulers over us? What have you done to us?"

They're not angry at the Philistines. They're angry at Samson for disturbing the peace. Israel has gotten so used to slavery that freedom looks like a threat.

And yet—and this is the amazing part—God acts anyway. He doesn't wait for Israel to cry out. He doesn't wait for them to repent. He starts working their deliverance even though they don't want it.

That's grace. Grace that shows up when we don't deserve it. Grace that pursues us even when we're not looking for it. Grace that refuses to give up on people who have given up on themselves.

THE MIRACLE BABY

God's rescue plan starts in an unlikely place: with a barren woman in an obscure village. "A certain man of Zorah, named Manoah, from the clan of the Danites, had a wife who was childless, unable to give birth."

We don't even know her name. She's just "Manoah's wife"—a nobody in a nothing town from a tribe that had already lost most of its territory. Barren. Invisible. Hopeless.

But this is exactly where God loves to start.

The Angel of the Lord appeared to her with stunning news: "You are barren and childless, but you are going to become pregnant and give birth to a son." He gave her specific instructions. She wasn't to drink wine or eat anything unclean. And the child would be special: "No razor may be used on his head, because the boy is to be a Nazirite, dedicated to God from the womb. He will begin to deliver Israel from the hands of the Philistines."

A Nazirite was someone set apart for God's special service. The Nazirite vow had three main requirements: no wine or grape products, no contact with dead bodies, and no cutting of the hair. These weren't random rules—they were outward signs of inward dedication. The uncut hair, in particular, was a visible symbol that this person belonged to God.

Notice something important: the angel said Samson would "begin" to deliver Israel. Not complete the deliverance—just begin it. From the very start, God knew Samson wouldn't finish the job. He would only start something that others would have to complete.

Manoah's wife told her husband what happened. Manoah prayed for the angel to come back—he wanted to hear the instructions himself. God graciously answered. The angel appeared again, confirmed everything, and then ascended in the flame of their offering. When Manoah realized they had seen God, he panicked: "We are doomed to die!"

But his wife—this unnamed woman who turns out to be wiser than her husband—calmly pointed out the obvious: "If the LORD had meant to kill us, he would not have accepted our offering or shown us all these things."

She was right. God wasn't coming to destroy them. He was coming to save them.

The baby was born. They named him Samson. "He grew and the LORD blessed him, and the Spirit of the LORD began to stir him." Everything was set up perfectly. Miraculous birth. Divine calling. The Spirit's power. Samson had every advantage.

Now watch what he does with it.

THE WOMAN IN TIMNAH

The first words out of adult Samson's mouth tell you everything you need to know about him. "I have seen a Philistine woman in Timnah; now get her for me as my wife." Not "I've met a godly woman." Not "I've found someone who shares my faith." Just "I saw her. I want her. Get her for me."

His parents objected. "Isn't there an acceptable woman among your relatives or among all our people? Must you go to the uncircumcised Philistines to get a wife?"

Good question. Israelites weren't supposed to marry Canaanites or Philistines. These marriages would lead to idolatry—which was exactly what had gotten Israel into trouble in the first place.

But Samson's answer was final: "Get her for me. She's the right one for me." Literally, the Hebrew says "she is right in my eyes." Remember that phrase—it's going to be important at the end of Judges.

Now here's where the story gets complicated. The narrator inserts an editorial comment: "His parents did not know that this was from the LORD, who was seeking an occasion to confront the Philistines."

Wait—God wanted this? Was God approving of Samson's bad choice?

Not exactly. God wasn't endorsing Samson's sinful desire. But God is so sovereign, so powerful, that he can use even our foolish decisions to accomplish his purposes. Samson was acting selfishly. God was working through Samson's selfishness to create conflict with the Philistines—conflict that Israel was too comfortable to start on their own.

This doesn't make Samson's choice right. It shows that God can bring good out of bad. That's not an excuse to make bad choices; it's a reminder that God is bigger than our mistakes.

RIDDLES AND REVENGE

On the way to Timnah, a lion attacked Samson. "The Spirit of the LORD came powerfully upon him so that he tore the lion apart with his bare hands."

That's our first glimpse of Samson's supernatural strength. He killed a lion like it was nothing—and then didn't even mention it to his parents.

Later, passing by the lion's carcass, Samson found that bees had made honey in it. He scooped out the honey and ate it. This might seem like a small detail, but it's actually significant. As a Nazirite, Samson wasn't supposed to touch dead bodies. By eating honey from a corpse, he was already compromising his vow.

At his wedding feast, Samson posed a riddle to the Philistine guests, betting them thirty sets of clothes: "Out of the eater, something to eat; out of the strong, something sweet."

The Philistines couldn't solve it. So they pressured Samson's bride: "Coax your husband into explaining the riddle for us, or we will burn you and your father's household to death."

For seven days she nagged him. She cried. She accused him of not loving her. Finally, worn down, Samson told her the answer. She told the Philistines.

Furious at being betrayed, Samson went to a Philistine town, killed thirty men, took their clothes to pay his debt, and stormed off. His wife was given to his best man.

Later, when Samson came back expecting to be with his wife and found out she'd been given away, his anger exploded again. He caught three hundred foxes, tied torches to their tails, and released them into the Philistine grain fields. The crops burned. The Philistines, in retaliation, burned Samson's wife and her father alive—the very thing they had threatened to do.

Samson responded with more violence. "He attacked them viciously and slaughtered many of them."

Do you see what's happening? It's an endless cycle of revenge. Someone hurts someone, who hurts someone back, who hurts someone else. There's no justice here—just anger and payback and more death.

And through it all, Samson never once thinks about God's mission. He never rallies Israel against the Philistines. He never tries to free his people. Every act of violence is personal revenge, not national deliverance.

BOUND BY HIS OWN PEOPLE

The Philistines demanded that Judah hand over Samson. So three thousand men from Judah—Samson's own people— went to arrest him.

Their words are devastating: "Don't you realize that the Philistines are rulers over us? What have you done to us?"

They weren't asking, "How can we help you fight?" They were asking, "Why are you making trouble?"

Samson let them tie him up. But when the Philistines came rushing toward him, "the Spirit of the LORD came powerfully upon him. The ropes on his arms became like charred flax, and the bindings dropped from his hands." He grabbed a donkey's jawbone and killed a thousand Philistines.

After the battle, Samson was dying of thirst. He called out to God: "You have given your servant this great victory. Am I now to die of thirst and fall into the hands of the uncircumcised?"

God opened up a spring, and Samson drank and was revived. This is the high point of Samson's career. A great victory. A prayer answered. For a moment, it looks like Samson might actually fulfill his calling.

"Samson led Israel for twenty years in the days of the Philistines." Twenty years. And that one sentence is all we get. The narrator skips over two decades to get to the part of the story that really matters—the part where everything falls apart.

GAZA AND DELILAH

"One day Samson went to Gaza, where he saw a prostitute. He went in to spend the night with her." That's it. No explanation. No excuse. The man set apart for God from the womb went to an enemy city and slept with a prostitute.

When the Philistines surrounded the city to trap him, Samson got up at midnight, ripped the city gates off their hinges, and carried them to a hilltop. It was an impressive display of strength—and a complete waste. He used his God-given power to escape the consequences of his sin, not to serve God's purposes.

Then came Delilah.

"Some time later, he fell in love with a woman in the Valley of Sorek whose name was Delilah." The Philistine rulers came to her with an offer: "See if you can lure him into showing you the secret of his great strength and how we can overpower him so we may tie him up and subdue him. Each one of us will give you eleven hundred shekels of silver." That's a massive sum—enough money to set Delilah up for life.

What followed was one of the most frustrating sequences in the entire Bible. Delilah asked Samson for the secret of his strength. He lied. She tried to subdue him. It didn't work. She accused him of not loving her. He lied again. Same result. Over and over this happened.

Any reasonable person would have seen what was happening. Delilah wasn't subtle. Every time Samson told her something, she immediately tried to use it against him. How many times does someone have to betray you before you stop trusting them?

But Samson was blind to it—blind long before the Philistines ever took his eyes. He was so obsessed, so controlled by his desires, that he couldn't see what was right in front of him.

Finally, "with such nagging she prodded him day after day until he was sick to death of it." Sound familiar? It's exactly what happened with his first wife. Samson never learned.

"So he told her everything. 'No razor has ever been used on my head,' he said, 'because I have been a Nazirite dedicated to God from my mother's womb. If my head were shaved, my strength would leave me, and I would become as weak as any other man.'"

Delilah called the Philistines. They came with the money. She lulled Samson to sleep on her lap, had a man shave off his hair, and began to subdue him.

"Then she called, 'Samson, the Philistines are upon you!'"

He woke up thinking he would escape as before.

"But he did not know that the LORD had left him."

Those might be the saddest words in the book. The Spirit of God, who had empowered Samson his whole life, was gone. And Samson didn't even notice. He had drifted so far, played with his gift for so long, that when God finally withdrew, Samson couldn't tell the difference.

The Philistines seized him, gouged out his eyes, and brought him to Gaza in bronze chains. The mighty warrior became a blind slave, grinding grain in prison.

THE FINAL ACT

But the story doesn't end there. "The hair on his head began to grow again."

The Philistines gathered to celebrate. Their god Dagon had delivered Samson into their hands—or so they believed. They filled their temple, packed the roof with spectators, and called for Samson to entertain them. The mighty judge of Israel had become a sideshow attraction for their amusement.

Samson asked the servant leading him to position him between the two central pillars that supported the temple. Then Samson prayed: "Sovereign LORD, remember me. Please,

God, strengthen me just once more, and let me with one blow get revenge on the Philistines for my two eyes."

It's a prayer—the second prayer in the whole Samson story. But notice what he prays for: revenge. Not for God's glory. Not for Israel's freedom. Revenge for his own eyes.

Even at the end, Samson was thinking about Samson.

But God answered anyway. Samson pushed against the pillars with all his might. The temple collapsed. Thousands of Philistines died—including all their rulers. "Thus he killed many more when he died than while he lived."

That sentence should make you pause. It's not a compliment. It's a tragedy. This man with the highest calling, the greatest gifts, the most potential—and he accomplished more in death than in twenty years of life.

WHAT THIS MEANS FOR US

What do we do with a story like this?

First, gifts don't guarantee faithfulness. Samson had more raw power than anyone in Israel's history. But strength without character is dangerous. Your talents, your abilities, your potential—none of it matters if you don't use it for God's purposes.

Second, slow drift leads to sudden collapse. Samson didn't fall overnight. He compromised his Nazirite vow piece by piece. He touched a dead lion. He partied at pagan feasts. He hung out with immoral friends. Each step seemed small at the time. But eventually, there was nothing left to compromise. The fall that looks sudden is usually the result of a thousand small surrenders.

Third, we can ignore God's warnings until it's too late. Delilah betrayed Samson three times before he told her the truth. How many warnings do we need? How many times does God have to show us the danger before we turn away?

Fourth, Samson is Israel in concentrated form. Everything wrong with Israel shows up in Samson. Miraculous calling, wasted potential. Drawn to foreign women like Israel was drawn to foreign gods. Blinded. Enslaved. Crying out to God only when there was nowhere else to turn. When Israel looked at Samson, they were supposed to see themselves.

Fifth, God still uses broken people. This is the mystery at the heart of the story. Samson failed spectacularly. And yet God still answered his prayer at the end. Being cast down doesn't mean being cast off. Even from the pit of our worst failures, we can still call on God.

But here's what Samson's story doesn't give us: a happy ending. The man who was supposed to deliver Israel only "began" the work. The Philistines were hurt but not defeated. The cycle wasn't broken.

Samson points us toward our need for a different kind of hero—one who won't waste his calling, who won't chase after foreign gods, who will finish what he starts. Samson's strength came and went. We need a savior whose power never fails.

TALKING POINTS

1. **Samson had every advantage—miraculous birth, divine calling, supernatural strength—and still failed.** Why do you think gifts and potential don't automatically lead to faithfulness?

2. **Samson's downfall came through small compromises that added up over time.** Can you think of examples where "small" choices led to big consequences?

3. **Delilah betrayed Samson over and over, but he kept trusting her.** Why do you think he couldn't see what was happening? What makes it hard for us to recognize danger in our own lives?

4. **Even at the end, Samson prayed for revenge rather than for God's glory.** What does his prayer tell us about his heart? What should he have prayed for?

5. **Despite everything, God still answered Samson's final prayer.** What does this tell us about God's character? Does it surprise you?

Samson died between the pillars of a pagan temple, buried under the rubble with his enemies.

His family came to get his body. They buried him in his father's tomb, back where the story began. The man who had wandered so far from his calling finally came home.

"He had led Israel twenty years." That's how it ends. No celebration. No peace. Just a quiet burial and a number. The strongest man who ever lived couldn't save Israel. The judges have all failed. The cycle is broken—not because Israel learned their lesson, but because there's no one left to deliver them.

We've now finished the stories of the judges. But the book isn't over. The final chapters show us just how dark things became when "everyone did what was right in their own eyes."

It's going to get worse before it gets better. Turn the page.

7

WHEN EVERYONE DOES THEIR OWN THING

Have you ever seen a knockoff toy? You know the kind—it looks almost like the real thing on the package. The colors are right. The shape is close. But when you open the box, something's off. The pieces don't fit together. The paint is sloppy. The joints break after five minutes. It says "LEGO" on the outside, but it's actually "LEBO" or "LEPIN" or something that's trying to fool you.

Knockoffs exist because somebody wanted the real thing but didn't want to pay the real price. So they made a cheap copy. And cheap copies never work as well as the original.

In Judges 17–18, we're going to watch an entire nation create knockoff religion. They don't want to worship the way God commanded. They don't want to go where God said to go. They don't want to follow the rules God gave them. So they make their own version—homemade gods, hired priests, DIY worship. It looks religious on the outside. It uses God's name. But it's fake. And fake religion, like fake toys, falls apart.

We've reached a new section of Judges. The stories of the judges are over. Samson is dead. The cycle of sin, oppression, crying out, and deliverance has ground to a halt—not because Israel finally learned their lesson, but because they've sunk so low they don't even want to be rescued anymore.

Now the writer is going to show us what Israel looked like from the inside. No more enemy armies. No more foreign oppressors. Just ordinary Israelites living ordinary lives—and the results are horrifying.

The refrain that echoes through these final chapters says it all: "In those days Israel had no king; everyone did what was right in their own eyes."

That sounds like freedom. It's actually chaos.

A MAN NAMED MICAH

The story begins with a man named Micah, who lived in the hill country of Ephraim. Here's how we meet him: "He said to his mother, 'The eleven hundred shekels of silver that were taken from you and about which I heard you utter a curse—I have that silver with me; I took it.'"

Wait—what? Our main character introduces himself by confessing that he stole a massive amount of money from his own mother. Eleven hundred shekels was a fortune. (Remember, that's exactly what each Philistine lord offered Delilah to betray Samson.) And Micah stole it from his mom.

Why is he confessing now? Because his mother had cursed whoever took the money, and Micah was afraid the curse would land on him. So he gave it back—not because stealing was wrong, but because he was scared of the consequences.

His mother's response? "The LORD bless you, my son!"

She tried to cancel the curse with a blessing. As if you could undo supernatural consequences with the right magic words. As if God's moral law worked like a spell you could reverse.

Then things got even stranger. The mother said, "I solemnly consecrate my silver to the LORD for my son to make an image overlaid with silver."

Do you see what's happening? She's dedicating money to the Lord—to make an idol. She's using God's name to do something God had explicitly forbidden.

The second commandment couldn't be clearer: "You shall not make for yourself an image in the form of anything in heaven above or on the earth beneath or in the waters below." This wasn't complicated. This wasn't ambiguous. God said don't make idols. Period.

But Micah's mother acted like she could worship God however she wanted. As long as she said "for the LORD," surely God wouldn't mind, right?

She took two hundred of the eleven hundred shekels (keeping the rest for herself, apparently) and had a silversmith make a carved image and a metal idol. And these went into Micah's house.

THE DIY SHRINE

Micah didn't stop with just an idol. He went all in. "Now this man Micah had a shrine, and he made an ephod and some household idols and installed one of his sons as his priest."

Let's count the violations:

First, Micah built his own shrine. God had commanded Israel to worship at "the place the LORD your God will choose"—which at this time was Shiloh, where the tabernacle stood. You weren't supposed to set up your own personal worship center in your backyard.

Second, he made an ephod. The ephod was a special priestly garment used for seeking God's guidance. Only the high priest was supposed to have one. Micah just … made one. For himself.

Third, he made household idols. These were like the "gods" that Rachel stole from her father Laban back in Genesis—objects used for sorcery and false worship. Totally forbidden.

Fourth, he made his own son a priest. Only descendants of Aaron were supposed to serve as priests. Micah wasn't from the tribe of Levi. His son wasn't qualified. But Micah "installed" him anyway, as if priesthood were a job you could just hand out.

Do you see the pattern? Micah wanted all the trappings of religion without any of the obedience. He wanted to feel spiritual without actually submitting to God's instructions. He built a knockoff worship system—something that looked religious but was entirely made up.

And then comes the verse that explains everything: "In those days Israel had no king; everyone did what was right in their own eyes."

There it is. The theme of these final chapters. No authority. No accountability. No standard outside yourself. Just "whatever feels right to me."

THE LEVITE FOR HIRE

Into this mess wandered a young man—a Levite from Bethlehem in Judah, looking for a place to stay.

Now, Levites were supposed to be Israel's spiritual leaders. They were the tribe set apart to serve God, to teach his law, to maintain proper worship. They didn't inherit land like the other tribes because God himself was their inheritance. The other tribes were supposed to support them so they could focus on ministry.

But this Levite was homeless and jobless, wandering around looking for opportunity. He ended up at Micah's house.

Micah saw a golden opportunity. A real Levite! That would make his homemade shrine so much more legitimate. He made the young man an offer: "Live with me and be my father and priest, and I'll give you ten shekels of silver a year, your clothes and your food."

The Levite agreed. He moved in, and Micah "installed" him as priest—the same word used when he installed his own son. You don't "install" a priest like you install an appliance. But that's how Micah thought about it. Plug in a Levite, and your shrine works better.

Micah was thrilled. "Now I know that the LORD will be good to me, since this Levite has become my priest."

That's magical thinking. Micah believed that having the right religious professional would guarantee God's blessing—regardless of whether his worship was actually what God wanted. He thought he could manipulate God with the right ingredients, like following a recipe. Add one Levite, stir in an ephod, and blessing will automatically result.

But you can't manipulate God. You can't force his hand with religious props. God isn't a vending machine where you insert the right coins and blessing drops out. He's a person—a King— who wants genuine love and obedience, not empty rituals.

Micah had a shrine, idols, an ephod, household gods, and now a Levite priest. He had everything except the one thing that mattered: actual faithfulness to God.

THE DANITES' PROBLEM

Meanwhile, the tribe of Dan had a problem. Way back in the book of Joshua, each tribe had been assigned territory in the Promised Land. Dan's allotment was in the central region, near the coast. But as we learned in Judges 1, the Danites failed to drive out the inhabitants. In fact, the Amorites "pressed the people of Dan back into the hill country" and wouldn't let them come down to the plain.

So Dan—one of the twelve tribes of Israel—was essentially homeless. They had an inheritance, but they'd never claimed it. They had a God-given portion, but they hadn't trusted God enough to take it.

Instead of repenting and asking God for help, the Danites decided to find somewhere else to live. They sent five warriors to scout out the land and find an easier target.

These scouts happened to stop at Micah's house. They recognized the young Levite (maybe by his accent) and asked him what he was doing there. When he explained his setup—"Micah has hired me and I am his priest"—they saw an opportunity.

"Please inquire of God to learn whether our journey will be successful."

The Levite answered: "Go in peace. Your journey has the LORD's approval."

But did it? Could this hired priest at an illegal shrine, using forbidden ephods and idols, actually speak for God? The

Danites wanted divine guidance, but they were asking the wrong person in the wrong place using the wrong methods. It was like asking a fortune teller for God's will.

The scouts continued north until they found a city called Laish. The people there were peaceful and unsuspecting, living far from anyone who might help them. Easy pickings.

The scouts returned with their report: "We have seen the land, and it is very good. Let's attack them! The land is spacious, and God has given it into your hands."

Notice how casually they invoked God's name. "God has given it into your hands." But God hadn't given them Laish. God had given them the territory down by the coast—the territory they'd been too afraid to take. They were claiming God's blessing on a plan God had never authorized.

THE THEFT

Six hundred armed Danites set out to conquer Laish. On the way, they stopped at Micah's house. The five scouts told the others about Micah's setup—the idols, the ephod, the household gods. "Now you know what to do," they said.

What followed was basically a home invasion. While the six hundred soldiers stood at the gate, the five scouts went inside and grabbed everything—the carved image, the ephod, the household idols, the metal idol. They just took it all.

The Levite priest watched in shock. "What are you doing?" he asked. Their answer was chilling: "Be quiet! Don't say a word. Come with us, and be our father and priest. Isn't it better that you serve a tribe and clan in Israel as priest rather than just one man's household?"

It was a job offer. A promotion. More prestige, more influence, a bigger congregation. And the Levite—this man who was supposed to be devoted to God—didn't hesitate. "The priest was very pleased. He took the ephod, the household gods and the idol and went along with the people."

He didn't care about Micah. He didn't care about loyalty or integrity. He cared about a better deal. The Danites offered him an upgrade, and he took it without a second thought.

This is what happens when religion becomes a career instead of a calling. When priests are hired hands instead of servants of God. When spiritual leadership goes to whoever makes the best offer.

"MY GODS WHICH I MADE"

When Micah realized what had happened, he gathered his neighbors and chased after the Danites. When he caught up to them, he shouted out his complaint.

The Danites turned around. "What's the matter with you that you called out your men to fight?"

Micah's answer is one of the most tragically absurd lines in the entire Bible:

"You took the gods I made, and my priest, and went away. What else do I have?"

Read that again. "The gods I made."

Do you hear how ridiculous that sounds? A god you made isn't a god at all. A god that can be carried off by thieves isn't worth worshiping. A god that fits in your pocket, that you can buy from a silversmith, that you need to protect instead of the other way around—that's not a god. That's an object.

The writer wants us to feel the absurdity. Micah is devastated because someone stole his religion. But his religion was worthless from the start because it was something he invented. You can't make a god. You can only receive the God who made you.

The Danites weren't sympathetic. "Don't argue with us, or some of the men may get angry and attack you, and you and your family will lose your lives."

It was a threat. Shut up or die. Micah had no choice. He turned around and went home—without his idols, without his priest, without his entire religious system. The thing he had built with such care was gone, stolen by people who didn't even pretend to be righteous.

THE CONQUEST OF LAISH

The Danites continued to Laish. The people there were peaceful and unsuspecting, living quietly, minding their own business. They had no army, no alliances, no defenses.

The Danites attacked and killed everyone. They burned the city to the ground. Then they rebuilt it and renamed it Dan, after their ancestor. "There they set up the idols for themselves, and Jonathan son of Gershom, the son of Moses, and his sons were priests for the tribe of Dan until the time of the captivity of the land."

Wait—did you catch that name? Jonathan, son of Gershom, son of Moses. The young Levite—the wandering priest-for-hire who served at Micah's illegal shrine and then happily transferred to the Danites' bigger operation—was a direct descendant of Moses himself.

Moses, the great lawgiver. Moses, who received the Ten

Commandments. Moses, who warned Israel again and again not to make idols or worship other gods. His own grandson (or great-grandson) ended up running a pagan worship center.

This is how far Israel had fallen. The rot reached all the way to the most honored family in the nation. Even Moses's descendants had abandoned Moses's God.

THE TRAGIC ENDING

The narrator closes with a devastating summary: "They continued to use the idols Micah had made, all the time the house of God was in Shiloh."

That last phrase is key. While Micah's stolen idols were being worshiped in Dan, the real house of God—the tabernacle, where God's presence actually dwelt—was standing in Shiloh. The legitimate place of worship was right there, available to anyone who wanted genuine relationship with God.

But the Danites preferred their knockoff. They wanted religion on their own terms, under their own control, shaped by their own preferences. The real thing was too demanding, too inconvenient, too far out of their hands.

This shrine at Dan would become one of the most destructive religious sites in Israel's history. Centuries later, when the kingdom split in two, King Jeroboam would set up golden calves at Dan (and Bethel), officially institutionalizing the very syncretism that started with Micah's silver idol. The shrine would stand until the Assyrians conquered the northern kingdom and carried the people into exile.

What started as one man's homemade religion became a nation's downfall.

WHAT THIS MEANS FOR US

This strange, disturbing story has more to teach us than we might expect.

First, doing what's right in your own eyes leads to chaos. The refrain of these chapters sounds like freedom—no rules, no restrictions, just follow your heart. But "follow your heart" is terrible advice when your heart is broken. Without an authority outside ourselves, we just wander deeper into our own confusion.

Second, sincerity doesn't make false worship acceptable. Micah seems genuinely religious. He dedicates silver to the Lord. He's thrilled to get a Levite priest. He's devastated when his gods are stolen. But sincerity without truth is just sincere error. You can be completely devoted to something completely wrong.

Third, religious professionals can be just as lost as everyone else. The Levite in this story should have known better. He was from the tribe set apart for God's service. But he was a hired hand, motivated by money and prestige, willing to serve at any shrine that paid his salary. A title doesn't guarantee faithfulness.

Fourth, success doesn't mean God approves. The Danites got what they wanted. They found a city, conquered it, established their shrine, and it lasted for generations. By worldly standards, they succeeded. But success and righteousness are not the same thing. Sometimes sin "works"—in the short term. God doesn't stop every bad plan. That doesn't mean he approves.

Fifth, we need more than religion—we need the right King. The problem in Judges wasn't just that Israel lacked a human king. They had rejected their divine King. They didn't want God to rule over them, so they made up their own rules, their own worship, their own gods. What Israel needed—what we all need—is to stop doing what's right in our own eyes and submit to the King who actually knows what's right.

TALKING POINTS

1. **Micah thought having a Levite priest guaranteed God's blessing.** What are some ways people today think they can guarantee God's favor through religious rituals or formulas?

2. **The Levite left Micah's service for a "better offer" from the Danites.** What does his choice reveal about his character? What should motivate people who serve God?

3. **Micah cried out, "You took the gods I made!"** Why is a "god you made" a contradiction? What are some "gods" people make for themselves today?

4. **The Danites' sin "succeeded"—they got their land and their shrine lasted for generations.** Why doesn't God always stop evil plans from working? How should we think about "success" in light of this story?

5. **The legitimate house of God at Shiloh was available the whole time.** Why do you think people preferred the knockoff religion at Dan? Why do people sometimes prefer their own version of faith to what God actually offers?

We've now seen Israel's religious collapse. A man makes his own gods. A priest sells his services. A tribe steals what they want and slaughters innocent people.

And remember: there's no enemy here. No Philistines, no Midianites, no foreign oppressors. This is just Israel being Israel. The cancer is inside.

But we haven't hit bottom yet. The next story is the darkest, most disturbing passage in the entire book—maybe in the entire Bible. It shows what happens when "everyone does what's right in their own eyes" in the most horrific way imaginable.

Steel yourself. Turn the page.

8

ROCK BOTTOM

Have you ever seen a situation spiral completely out of control?

Maybe it started with something small—a misunderstanding, a harsh word, a shove in the hallway. But then someone retaliated. And then the other side hit back harder. And before anyone knew what was happening, a small conflict had exploded into something terrible. People got hurt who had nothing to do with the original problem. By the end, everyone was asking, "How did we get here?"

In *The Lord of the Flies*, a group of boys stranded on an island start out trying to build a civilized society. They have rules. They have a leader. But slowly, as the boys stop listening to anyone but themselves, things fall apart. Small disagreements become violent conflicts. Fear and anger take over. By the end of the book, the island is on fire and children are dead. What started as an adventure became a nightmare—not because of any outside enemy, but because of what was inside the boys all along.

Judges 19–21 is like that. It's the darkest story in the entire book—maybe the darkest story in the entire Bible.

It starts with a family argument. It ends with civil war, mass slaughter, and the near-destruction of an entire tribe of Israel. Along the way, you'll meet some of the most despicable characters in Scripture and watch God's people sink to depths that rival the worst pagan nations.

This is not a comfortable chapter to read. But it's an important one. Because the writer wants us to see exactly where "everyone doing what's right in their own eyes" ultimately leads. He wants us to stare into the abyss and understand why Israel so desperately needed a King.

Take a deep breath. Let's go.

A LEVITE AND HIS CONCUBINE

The story begins, as always: "In those days Israel had no king." A Levite living in the hill country of Ephraim had a concubine—a secondary wife with fewer legal rights than a full wife. She was from Bethlehem in Judah. Something went wrong between them (the text suggests she was angry with him), and she left, going back to her father's house. She stayed there for four months.

Eventually, the Levite went to bring her back. Her father was thrilled to see him—a reconciliation meant the family's honor was restored. The father-in-law was so hospitable that he kept convincing the Levite to stay "just one more day." Day after day, the two men ate and drank together while the woman waited.

Finally, late on the fifth day, the Levite insisted on leaving. But because of all the delays, they couldn't make it home before dark. They were near Jebus (the city that would later become

Jerusalem), and the Levite's servant suggested they stop there for the night.

The Levite refused. "We won't go into any city whose people are not Israelites. We will go on to Gibeah."

Do you hear the assumption? Foreign cities were dangerous. Israelite cities were safe. The Levite trusted his own people.

He was tragically wrong.

NO ROOM IN GIBEAH

They arrived at Gibeah, a town in the territory of Benjamin, and sat down in the city square. In the ancient world, travelers expected someone to offer hospitality. It was a sacred duty. You didn't leave strangers sleeping in the street.

But no one in Gibeah invited them in.

Think about that. The writer has just shown us the Levite's father-in-law in Bethlehem, who was so generous he practically begged his guests to stay. Now we see Gibeah, where the townspeople walked right past these travelers without offering so much as a meal. The contrast is deliberate. Something is deeply wrong in this Israelite town.

Finally, an old man came in from working in the fields. He wasn't originally from Gibeah—he was from Ephraim, just living there. When he saw the travelers in the square, he asked where they were going and where they came from.

The Levite explained their situation and added, "We have straw and fodder for our donkeys and bread and wine for ourselves. We don't need anything."

The old man insisted: "Don't spend the night in the square. Come to my house."

It was the only offer of hospitality they received—and it came from an outsider, not a native of Gibeah.

SODOM IN ISRAEL

What happened next echoes one of the most infamous stories in the Bible.

While they were enjoying the evening, wicked men from the city surrounded the house. They pounded on the door and shouted to the old man: "Bring out the man who came to your house so we can hurt him."

If this sounds familiar, it should. It's almost word-for-word what happened in Genesis 19, when the men of Sodom surrounded Lot's house and demanded he hand over his angelic visitors. Sodom was destroyed by fire from heaven for its wickedness.

Now the same evil had taken root in Israel. The writer wants us to feel the horror: Gibeah has become a new Sodom—except this Sodom is populated by God's own people.

The old man went out and pleaded with the mob: "No, my friends, don't be so vile. Since this man is my guest, don't do this outrageous thing."

Then he made a terrible offer—so terrible it's hard to read. He offered to send out his own virgin daughter and the Levite's concubine instead.

The mob refused. They wanted the man.

What happened next reveals the Levite's true character. He grabbed his concubine and shoved her outside. The text says simply: "He sent her outside to them."

He sacrificed her to save himself.

The wicked men of Gibeah abused her throughout the

night, treating her with unspeakable cruelty. When dawn came, they let her go. She collapsed at the doorway of the house, her hands on the threshold, and didn't move.

In the morning, the Levite opened the door, ready to continue his journey as if nothing had happened. He found her lying there.

"Get up," he said. "Let's go."

There was no answer. She was dead—or nearly so.

He put her on his donkey and went home.

THE LEVITE'S MESSAGE

What the Levite did next was shocking in a different way. He took a knife and cut his concubine's body into twelve pieces. Then he sent those pieces throughout the territory of Israel.

It was a gruesome summons, a horrifying call to action. The message was clear: Look what happened in Israel. What are you going to do about it?

Everyone who saw it said, "Such a thing has never been seen or done, not since the day the Israelites came up out of Egypt. Just imagine! We must do something! So speak up!"

The nation was outraged. Four hundred thousand armed men gathered at Mizpah to hear what had happened and decide what to do.

But here's something important to notice: the Levite told his story in a way that made himself look innocent. He said the men of Gibeah "came after me and surrounded the house, intending to kill me." He didn't mention that he was the one who threw his concubine outside. He presented himself as a victim, not a coward who sacrificed a woman to save his own skin.

The truth was twisted. And based on that twisted truth, Israel prepared for war.

CIVIL WAR

The Israelites sent messengers throughout the tribe of Benjamin: "What about this awful crime that was committed among you? Now turn over those wicked men of Gibeah so that we may put them to death."

It was a reasonable demand. The guilty should be punished. Justice should be served.

But the Benjaminites refused. They chose to protect their own, even when their own had committed monstrous evil. Instead of handing over the guilty men, they mobilized for war—26,000 soldiers, plus 700 elite fighters from Gibeah itself.

Benjamin chose solidarity with Sodom.

The Israelites sought God's guidance at Bethel, where the ark of the covenant was located. "Who should go first to fight against Benjamin?"

God answered: "Judah shall go first."

So Israel attacked—and lost. Benjamin cut down 22,000 Israelites that first day.

The Israelites wept before the LORD and asked again: "Shall we go up again to fight Benjamin our brother?"

God answered: "Go up against them."

The second day, Benjamin killed another 18,000 Israelites.

This is confusing, isn't it? Israel was seeking justice. They asked God what to do, and God told them to fight. Yet they kept losing. Forty thousand Israelites died in two days.

What was happening?

Israel, despite being on the right side of this particular conflict, was not as righteous as they thought. They had their own sins. They had tolerated evil in their midst for years. Now, even as they punished Benjamin's sin, they were being purified by fire themselves.

On the third day, Israel fasted and offered sacrifices. Phinehas the priest (grandson of Aaron himself—this was early in the period of the judges) stood before the ark and asked: "Shall we go up again to fight Benjamin our brother, or not?" God answered: "Go, for tomorrow I will give them into your hands."

This time, Israel set an ambush. They drew Benjamin's army out of the city, then struck from behind. The trap worked. Benjamin's forces were routed. Only 600 men escaped, fleeing to a rock called Rimmon where they hid for four months.

But Israel wasn't finished. They went through all the towns of Benjamin, killing everyone—men, women, children, livestock. They burned every town to the ground.

The tribe of Benjamin was nearly wiped from existence.

A PROBLEM OF THEIR OWN MAKING

With the battle over, Israel suddenly realized what they had done. They had sworn an oath at Mizpah: "Not one of us will give his daughter in marriage to a Benjaminite." It seemed righteous at the time—Benjamin had sided with violent criminals. Why should they be allowed to marry Israelite women?

But now only 600 Benjaminite men remained. No wives meant no children. No children meant the tribe would disappear within a generation. Israel had essentially condemned Benjamin to extinction.

The people gathered at Bethel and wept. "LORD, God of Israel, why has this happened? Why should one tribe be missing from Israel today?"

It's a strange prayer. They were the ones who had made the oath. They were the ones who had slaughtered Benjamin's women and children. Now they acted as if this tragedy had just happened to them, as if God were responsible for the mess they had created.

But they couldn't—or wouldn't—break their oath. So they looked for loopholes.

First, they remembered another oath: anyone who hadn't come to the assembly at Mizpah would be put to death. They checked the roll and discovered that no one from Jabesh-Gilead had come.

So they sent twelve thousand soldiers to Jabesh-Gilead with instructions to kill everyone except young unmarried women. They found four hundred young women and brought them back for the Benjaminite survivors.

Four hundred women. Six hundred men. They were still two hundred short.

Someone came up with another plan. Every year there was a festival at Shiloh where young women came out to dance in the vineyards. The elders told the remaining Benjaminites: "Go and hide in the vineyards, and when the young women of Shiloh come out to dance, rush out and each of you seize one of them to be your wife."

If anyone complained, the elders had a ready excuse: "Do us a favor. You didn't technically give your daughters to Benjamin—they were taken. So you haven't broken your oath!"

It was kidnapping. It was wrong. But it solved the problem, so everyone went along with it.

The narrator's verdict is devastating: "In those days Israel had no king; everyone did what was right in his own eyes."

WHAT JUST HAPPENED?

Let's step back and trace the chain of disasters:

- A Levite treats his concubine badly enough that she leaves him
- Delays keep them traveling late, forcing them to stop in Gibeah
- The men of Gibeah commit an unspeakable crime
- The Levite sacrifices his concubine to save himself, then mutilates her body
- Israel gathers for war based on the Levite's self-serving account
- Benjamin protects the guilty instead of surrendering them
- Civil war erupts, killing tens of thousands
- Israel nearly exterminates an entire tribe
- To fix the problem they created, Israel destroys Jabesh-Gilead
- To finish fixing it, they authorize the kidnapping of innocent girls

Every step made things worse. Evil multiplied evil. One sin led to another, then another, until the whole nation was drenched in blood.

And notice: there are no Canaanites in this story. No Philistines, no Midianites, no foreign oppressors. This is Israel destroying Israel. The enemy was never really outside. It was inside all along.

WHAT THIS MEANS FOR US

This is a brutal story. What could it possibly teach us?

First, sin escalates. What started as a family dispute ended in civil war and mass kidnapping. Small evils, left unchecked, grow into catastrophes. The Levite's callousness toward his concubine was a symptom of deeper rot—and that rot eventually consumed an entire nation.

Second, "doing what's right in your own eyes" leads to horror. Everyone in this story thought they were justified. The men of Gibeah wanted what they wanted. The Levite protected himself. Benjamin defended their tribe. Israel executed justice (or so they thought). Everyone had reasons. Everyone was right in their own eyes. And the result was unspeakable evil.

Third, religious activity doesn't guarantee righteousness. Israel went to Bethel. They inquired of the Lord. They offered sacrifices. They had the ark and the high priest. But all their religious motions didn't prevent them from slaughtering their own brothers, destroying a city to steal wives, and authorizing kidnapping. You can go through all the right rituals and still have a heart far from God.

Fourth, twisted truth leads to twisted justice. The Levite's selective account shaped Israel's response. He hid his own guilt and presented himself as a pure victim. When we distort the truth—even to make ourselves look better—we distort everything that follows.

Fifth, we need a King. The refrain pounds like a heartbeat through these final chapters: "In those days Israel had no king." The writer isn't just making a historical observation. He's crying out for what Israel desperately needed—not just any king, but a righteous king who would establish justice, protect the vulnerable, and lead the people in God's ways.

That King was coming.

But first, Israel had to hit rock bottom.

TALKING POINTS

1. **The Levite threw his concubine to the mob to save himself.** What does his action reveal about his character? How does selfishness lead to cruelty?

2. **Benjamin chose to protect guilty men rather than hand them over for justice.** Why do you think they made that choice? When is loyalty to "our own people" actually wrong?

3. **Israel kept seeking God's guidance but still suffered terrible losses.** What might God have been teaching them through those defeats? Does asking God for guidance guarantee everything will go smoothly?

4. **To solve the problem they created, Israel destroyed Jabesh-Gilead and kidnapped women from Shiloh.** How did their "solution" create more victims? What happens when we try to fix our mistakes with more sin?

5. **The refrain says "everyone did what was right in his own eyes."** How is this different from actually doing what's right? Why do we need an authority outside ourselves?

THE END—AND THE BEGINNING

The book of Judges ends here, in the smoking ruins of a nation that has torn itself apart. No triumphant victory. No wise leader rising to restore order. Just a final, weary statement: "In those days Israel had no king; everyone did what was right in his own eyes."

We've traveled a long road through this book. We watched Israel fail to complete the conquest, then slowly drift into the worship of false gods. We saw God raise up judges—flawed, broken people who won temporary victories but couldn't change Israel's heart. We witnessed the spiral downward: Gideon's ephod, Abimelech's violence, Jephthah's vow, Samson's self-destruction. And now this—civil war, massacre, kidnapping, a nation in ruins.

The book of Judges is not a story of heroes. It's a story of failure. It's a mirror that shows us what happens when people abandon God and trust themselves instead.

But it's also a story of grace. Because somehow, impossibly, Israel survived. God didn't destroy them, even when they deserved it. He kept working, kept waiting, kept preparing for something better.

Israel needed a King. Not just a human king—though that was coming—but *the* King. One who would perfectly obey where Israel had perfectly failed. One who would save not just from enemies outside but from the enemy within. One who wouldn't just begin deliverance, like Samson, but would complete it forever. That King was coming.

But first, there would be more darkness, more waiting, more longing for the dawn.

The story continues in 1 Samuel, where a barren woman will pray, a boy will hear God's voice in the night, and a shepherd will rise to take the throne.

Keep reading. The best is yet to come.